A Lifetir
On The Buses

Jim Sambrooks

ISBN 9781905304066

Contents

All photographs are by the author unless otherwise credited.

(Front Cover)
Preserved Yorkshire Traction 492, HE 6762, a Leyland Tiger TS7 with Weymann bodywork. The chassis was new in April 1935 and rebodied in April 1950.
-

(Back Cover)
Jim Sambrooks is seen in Doncaster with Doncaster 22 in May 2002 promoting the forthcoming centenary celebrations of public transport in Doncaster. (Bob Ashton)

(Title Page)
London Transport RT1548, KGU 440, with Park Royal body may have been one of the buses which came to Hertford garage for steam-cleaning or repainting. It was new in September 1949 as a red bus and was allocated to Hounslow. It emerged from Aldenham, following overhaul in 1964, in green livery and then was sent to Harlow, where it is shown operating a town service. It passed to the newly created London Country in January 1970.

This story which has also been published in 'Historic Commercial News,' the magazine of the Historic Commercial Vehicle Society, and I'm proud to say it won their literary award for two years running.

Chapter One – Early Days

This was to be 'my life on the buses' and it will develop into that but first I thought I'd share some of my early memories which, possibly, influenced me into wanting to work on the buses. I've never been any good at remembering dates and in any case, some stories cover a number of years so the following is not in any particular order. I should say from the beginning that these notes are from my memory, up to sixty years ago, so details should not be read as factually correct.

I was born in Sunderland in 1950, the first of four children. My parents always said my first spoken word was "bus" and I would point them out from my push-chair. That love of buses has stayed with me. The only job I wanted was a bus driver's and I've now reached retirement age after nearly fifty years in the industry.

We lived with my paternal grandparents for the first three years of my life. It was a large council house on a corner of North Hylton Road in Southwick, a village that had been overtaken by the spread of the town. Maternal grandparents lived at the other end of the same village. On the opposite side of North Hylton Road was a large factory and I was always fascinated by the buses that queued up for the workers at home time, the Northern General Transport Co (Northern) had some double-deckers with starting handles whilst the Sunderland Corporation Transport Department (Corporation) had some centre-entrance double-deckers. All were half-cab, of course, back-loaders being the norm.

When I was three years old we moved out of the grandparents' house into a new council house on the developing Hylton Castle Estate, further out of town on the same road. Shortly after the move I was admitted to hospital for tonsil removal, I remember the long ward with a coal fire at the end and wanting to go home in a green ambulance. Unfortunately, the green ambulances belonged to Durham County Council so I had to make do with a Corporation cream one.

The route to our estate, the 17, was jointly worked by the Corporation and Northern, the latter also passing the estate on two routes to Newcastle, the 22 and the 64, and a route to Brady Square, and if such a bus was to take us home I would get very excited and announce that we were going on a Brady Square bus. "How do you know?" asked the parents before it was close enough to read the blind. "It's a pointy bus" would be my reply and I was always right. Dad related this tale many times over the years and on seeing a wartime utility trolleybus at Sandtoft he told me it was a pointy bus like the buses that ran to Brady Square. A letter to Geoff Burrows at Classic Bus magazine proved the point, Northern used utility buses on that route! We once visited Brady Square to see what was there; all I remember is a long footbridge over a railway marshalling yard at the back of Washington chemical works.

Northern tickets always bore the legend 'Northern and Associated Companies' and these subsidiaries were listed on the back of the ticket including; Gateshead and District, Sunderland District, Tynemouth and District, Tyneside and Wakefield's. Naturally, I wanted to find all of these companies; the Sunderland District Omnibus Company (SDO) was easy as they ran out of the town using a lovely dark blue and white livery. Gateshead's maroon buses were seen as we passed through the town on our way to Newcastle. Tyneside ran along the north bank of the Tyne between Newcastle and North Shields in a dark green livery. Tynemouth and Wakefield's seemed to be one operator with two names and ran along the coast between North Shields, Tynemouth and Whitley Bay using red and cream buses.

Sunderland Corporation replaced its trams in 1954 and Dad took me for a last ride, I still remember asking why that 'bus' stopped in the middle of the road. A large fleet of new buses entered service, introducing a new green and cream livery. They were Daimler and Guy double-deckers with Gardner 5LW engines and bodies by Roe, Crossley or Associated Coachbuilders. Tale at the time was that a painter had turned up one day and asked what colour the bus should be, the foreman was called Green so said painter was told to see Green and that was the colour he used. A few centre-entrance double-deckers retained the old crimson livery awaiting withdrawal; imagine my delight when one of those turned up for the return from the grandparents one day.

When it was time for me to start school the infants hadn't been built on our estate so I was put on a Corporation bus to a school in Roker. I loved going to school and loved going home again, it was just the bit in between I wasn't keen on. When the infant's school opened on our estate I would walk unaccompanied after the first day and once or twice a week would catch a bus from outside the school to visit grandparents. I would be escorted to the bus stop for my return journey. Once, in thick fog, the conductor sat on the front wing and directed the driver at about walking pace. I thought this was great as I didn't have to pay my fare.

Northern had a depot in the town centre, next to Park Lane bus station, and if the pocket money allowed I would go after school to watch the buses pull in, be fuelled, washed and parked up. The building was small and buses would be parked overnight in the bus station and surrounding streets.

Northern was an early convert to the Leyland Atlantean and these were seen on the routes to Newcastle. The Corporation tried a rear-engined demonstrator and this was used on the 17 route. I was so excited about this I told my junior school teacher, he told me to find out if it was an 'Atlantic' or a 'Fleetliner'. I should have been very impressed by this but I just thought teachers knew about such things. I was fortunate enough to catch this to the grandparents that day but the conductor didn't know what it was. I now know the Corporation tried a Daimler Fleetline demonstrator registered 7000 HP and painted blue and cream.

Like all good parents, mine sent me to Sunday school in a hall on our estate, but I was soon banished from this as I wouldn't sing. I then attended a Sunday school in Southwick where they didn't mind me not singing. To get there and back involved a bus ride so this suited me.

When staying with mother's parents, the bedroom overlooked Beaumont, pronounced 'Bew-mont', Street served by the Corporation's No 4 and 5 routes to Red House Estate (the Northern buses took a different route to Red House and were numbered 6A and 6B, simply because the buses only had two track number blinds and over a hundred routes were operated by then). The curtains were always left open so I could watch the drunks going past at closing time, probably about 10.30pm. I'll never know if that was meant to deter me from alcohol but it might have had the opposite effect. Perhaps I thought the drunks looked happy and decided to try it when I was old enough, who knows? Of course, I'd no interest in the drunks but every interest in the 4's and 5's.

Nana Chapelow had many daft sayings, some of which I still use such as "it's not far to walk if you run". If we misbehaved we would be threatened with "what Marley's cat got" we never dared misbehave again so never found out what Marley's cat actually got. "If I come over there I'll be beside you" was a real frightener. "A black eye with a whitening brush" was another. I often say to the junior members at Sandtoft when they get filthy helping me underneath trolleybuses "Your Mam will come down here and give me a black eye with a whitening brush". I once asked one of the lads what his mam would do to me when he went home filthy, the reply was "she hasn't got a wire brush so you won't get a black eye". Needless to say nobody ever got a black eye, with a whitening brush or anything else. Further down Beaumont Street was a Catholic Church with a statue overlooking the road. We had to be on our best behaviour when passing this as 'Holy Jo' was watching us.

Dad and granddad were keen supporters of Sunderland football club. This never rubbed off on me as I've never had any interest in any sort of sport. I would very occasionally allow them to take me as there was a special route to Roker Park on which the Corporation would run anything that moved. I once asked if I could go home as soon we reached the ground; a thick ear ensured I never asked again. There was an interesting part of the afternoon though, when all the footballers left the field and a brass band came on. When I was required to play football at school I would stand still and if the ball came towards me I would move out of its way.

When the senior school was built it was just off the estate but easy walking distance from our house. No buses were run at the beginning or end of the day but three buses left the school at dinnertime and only two returned. If I spotted an interesting bus on the outward trip I would dash off to the other end of the estate after dinner to catch it back to school, it was usually that one that had run off! The school was called Hylton Castle Secondary Modern and this must be the nearest I've ever been to modern in my life.

Days Out

Northern ran a route from our estate to South Shields, the 4A, where I discovered some funny blue buses with sticks on their roofs, very strange as they had full fronts and were very quiet. Dad explained that they

Sunderland 242 (CBR 539) 1952 Guy Arab IV/Roe seen in Fulwell depot in 1970 after the conversion to training bus. This was the only bus in the fleet fitted with Cave-Brown-Cave heating system, it subsequently passed into preservation with the North East Bus Preservation Group.

Northern 1639 (CU 7639) 1955 Guy Arab IV/Metro-Cammell in Park Lane bus station, Sunderland.

It is quite likely that during my visits to South Shields I would have observed 204, although not necessarily on learner duties. What I could not imagine is the fact that in 1970 it would arrive at Sandtoft and would undertake a complete restoration. *(Tony Belton)*

South Shields 232 was the penultimate new trolleybus delivered before the war and is viewed from the upper saloon of another South Shields trolleybus. *(Tony Belton)*

As a result of the closure of the small Pontypridd UDC trolleybus system in 1957, all the remaining vehicles passed to other operators. South Shields obtained four and this 1946 example, a Karrier W with Park Royal body, became 236. Two other Pontypridd trolleybuses passed to Doncaster Corporation where they were fitted with new bodies by Roe before they entered service. *(Tony Belton)*

The market place in South Shields was the hub of the system, all services bar one passing through. Operating on service 4, which would return to the Market Place as service 3, South Shields 249 was a Karrier W with Roe bodywork. *(Tony Belton)*

Despite my uncertainty in the text, Newcastle trolleybuses did serve the race course, service 31 reaching it at Gosforth Park. In the photograph above, BUT 9641T 485 with Metro-Cammell body (virtually identical to London Transport's Q1 class) is seen in the city centre in Grainger Street, while in the picture below, Sunbeam S7 527 with locally built Northern Coachbuilders body is at the aforementioned terminus at Gosforth. *(Tony Belton)*

Economic 8 (VUP 472) a 1957 AEC Reliance/Roe in Park Lane, Sunderland in 1973. Binns Bakery behind the bus supplied Binns shops as advertised on many buses throughout the north east.

Lockey, St Helens Auckland (JXN 378) a 1949 Leyland 7RT/Park Royal ex-London Transport, seen in Bishop Auckland in 1970. These black buses astonished me as a child, never having even imagined that buses could be painted black.

were trolleybuses and ran on electricity taken from the overhead wires. It always amazed me how the bus, the poles and the wires all passed under the station bridge. I now believe the wires splayed out and dipped to roof level. 'Shields soon became a favourite destination for me; I would ride on the trolleys while the family sat on the beach.

Parents obviously hadn't done their homework when we took a day trip to Holy Island, reached by train, steam of course, to a station called 'Beal for Holy Island'. I can't remember how we crossed the causeway to the island but we had to go straight back as the tide was turning and we would have been marooned for some time. Again I can't remember how we left the island but remember waiting for a bus to Berwick which turned out to be a rear-entrance single-decker. I occupied the seat behind the door. It would have been a United Bristol L. Mam bought tickets for the train back to Beal to continue on our return tickets. At that time all railway tickets were handed in at the end of the journey, it worried me greatly that our Berwick to Beal tickets weren't handed in.

One day, when Mam and sisters had gone to the pictures, Dad offered me a trip to Bishop Auckland by a 57 bus, a route jointly operated by United, Northern and Sunderland District. The latter was never referred to by its name; they were always 'the blue buses'. In 'Bishop, as it was locally known, I found black buses belonging to Lockey's, a firm called 'OK' with all sorts of fascinating buses and there were several other bus companies, Bond Bros with blue ones, G&B with brown ones and more.

A family day out saw us visit Newcastle races, reached by a 22 or a 64 then, I think, by trolleybus to the racecourse. I expect somebody will tell me trolleybuses never ran to the racecourse so that theory will be blown. In Newcastle our buses would arrive in Worswick, pronounced 'Wossick', Street bus station which sloped, the first thing the conductor would do when the bus stopped was to put a chock behind a wheel then remove it again as the bus pulled away. In the toilets I noticed that the porcelain was made in Newcastle but Dad was quick to explain that would have been another town of the same name in Staffordshire. On a different trip to Newcastle a Northern half-cab single-decker arrived instead of the expected double-decker and I was delighted. I think it was a Guy.

Another day out for the family was to Barnard Castle. We boarded a Durham District green bus, not from the bus station but from a back street nearby. I think.it was a back-loader single-decker, probably a Bristol L as Durham District Services was a subsidiary of United.

A railway excursion took us to the Lake District and a fleet of Ribble of double-deckers awaited our train, some of these had their entrance just behind the front wheel. I'd never seen this layout as it wasn't used on any of the fleets in the north east so I insisted on waiting for one of these.

Visiting relatives in Stockton on Tees and Middlesbrough meant travelling by a No 40 bus from Sunderland, another United, Northern, Sunderland District joint route. The route was Newcastle-Sunderland-West Hartlepool-Stockton-Middlesbrough but United didn't run north of Sunderland nor Northern & SDO south of West Hartlepool. I would marvel at the maroon-painted West Hartlepool Corporation buses as we passed through the town but one day noticed a blue bus belonging to Hartlepool Corporation. A trip had to be organised so that I could investigate these. It turned out that there were two municipal bus operators next to each other. Travelling south from Sunderland on the 40 meant paying to the village of Easington Lane and receiving a Northern ticket whosever bus it was then the same conductor coming round again collecting fares for the rest of the journey and issuing a United ticket.

Stockton had its own Corporation buses in a dark green livery whilst, at the far end of the 40 route, was Middlesbrough with Corporation buses in dark blue. Stockton routes were numbers in the conventional manner but Middlesbrough routes were lettered, the joint route between the two towns being numbered 0 or lettered O accordingly. One thing I noticed about Middlesbrough's blinds was that the letter O was always perfectly round, sometimes looking out of proportion to the other letters.

In Middlesbrough was the Transporter Bridge and, of course, I had to travel across the River Tees on it. At its north landing I discovered a West Hartlepool Corporation bus bound for its home town so now a round trip could be made. West Hartlepool was never known as such, usually abbreviated to 'West'.

A regular outing out for all the family was to walk to North Hylton where we would visit the Ferryboat Inn. There was a long room with a bar down one side. We would drink pop and eat those new-fangled things called crisps. A hand-rown ferry would be summoned to cross the River Wear. We would then walk up the hill into South Hylton and catch a 'Jolly bus' towards the town. W H Jolly ran a fleet of Bedford buses from their home village to the Infirmary, on the edge of the town, from where it was necessary to continue on a Corporation bus to the centre. Incidentally, when the Borough boundary was extended many years later Jolly was granted the licence to run through to the town centre. Otherwise we would walk along the south bank to Fatfield and board a bus either back to town or in the opposite direction to Washington where the bus station contained long concrete shelters which we kids would run up and down. The 22 and 64 served this bus station and would get us home.

From nearby Boldon we would catch a Northern bus to Jarrow on route 60 then walk through the pedestrian tunnel under the River Tyne. Halfway through the tunnel signs marked the boundaries of County Durham and Northumberland a few feet apart, we would rush to stand in 'no man's land' as Dad called it. From Hebburn we caught a green bus of the delightfully named Tyneside Tramways and Tramroads Company; I knew this was their title as it was spelt out on the tickets. This took us to North Shields after which we re-crossed the river by ferry to South Shields then caught a Northern 4A bus back to Hylton Castle or an Economic bus to Sunderland via the coast road.

Holidays

When I was about four years old Dad took me for a boating holiday on the Norfolk Broads, leaving Mam to look after my two sisters. I don't remember much about the boat but I do remember travelling on brown double-deckers. Brown single-deckers ran for the Economic Bus Company at home but brown double-deckers!!! Dad pointed out a sign on the bus saying it was built in Lowestoft, how about that? Brown double-deckers built in the town I was in!!! They were, of course, Lowestoft Corporation buses bodied by Eastern Coachworks (ECW). Back home shortly afterwards we boarded a United bus and spotted the same sign, it was a Bristol bodied by ECW. Sunderland Corporation had a batch of double-deckers bodied by Associated Coachbuilders in the town but this wasn't advertised so I didn't know about that or, perhaps, they hadn't been delivered by then.

An early family holiday was to Ovingham in Northumberland where the caravan was a converted bus, one of many in a field. I revisited the site many years later, in 1978 in fact, when only one bus remained. From my photograph Tony Peart identified it as a Leyland Lion.

We had a lot of relatives in the London area and, depending on which grandparents took me, the journey would be by coach or train. The United coaches wore a swooping green and cream livery with Tyne-Tees-Thames-Service on the quarter lights. They would travel through Doncaster and my granddad hated the place, he said you would queue for ages to get into the town, stop for an hour's break then queue to get out again. No by-pass in those days, the A1 ran through the town centre. To avoid this delay we often travelled overnight and were given a brown rug with the initials 'UAS' (United Automobile Services) embroidered in a corner, somebody once asked how many such rugs were in my possession, none of course, they had to be left on the coach.

On the way back the coach would pull into a petrol station and fill up. I didn't know diesel existed then. It always puzzled me how the drivers (there were always two on board) paid for this as they didn't collect any fares! Another trick they had was to change over without stopping the coach; one would slide out of the seat as the other slid in from the opposite side. The journey took twelve hours each way in what I now know to be Bristol LS coaches. I was overwhelmed by the number and variety of coaches at Victoria Coach Station in London, seemingly every combination of colours imaginable

My maternal granddad worked for the railway so the journey with them would be by train, much faster but nowhere near as interesting to me. Incidentally, we were told that granddad's job was to polish the rails and we were always encouraged to look out for rusty rails so granddad could go out and polish them. He was, in fact, a platelayer.

We would visit an aunt and uncle near Watford and alight the bus at Garston LT Garage as it said on the destination blind, the buses looked very old to me but they would have been RT type double-deckers designed in the 1930's and built up 'til 1954. They were country buses in London Transport's green and cream livery. Little did I know that one day I would be maintaining such buses? On one visit to Uncle

As mentioned in the text, visits to relatives in Colindale in north London afforded the opportunity to see the final withdrawn London trolleybuses in the scrapyard located there. In the upper picture, a line of all-Leyland K1 and K2 classes, latterly operated by Isleworth depot, await their fate. In the lower photograph it is the turn of chassis-less AECs of class L3, which were bodied by Metro-Cammell and which finally operated at Fulwell depot, and which closed the system in May 1962. *(Tony Belton)*

Ron's I was shown the beginnings of a new road that they said would link London with Sunderland without any cross roads or roundabouts, surely that would be impossible! It was, of course, early stages of the M1 being built; my cousin and I would play on the site after the workmen had gone home so playing on the motorway was accomplished and I lived to tell the tale.

Aunty Yvonne lived in Colindale in north London and a yard full of scrap trolleybuses greeted us from the train. I was told that all London's trolleybuses were out of service now and these were awaiting their fate.

We once spent a week in Eyemouth, just over the Scottish border. One day we visited Edinburgh where I was promised some trams. Luck wasn't on our side as they'd been recently replaced so I had to make do with a trip to the zoo.

My last holiday with the family was taken at Haydon Bridge in Northumberland. I was about 13 at the time and would travel to Hexham by a very old-looking purple double-decker belonging to North Tyne Transport whilst the others took the more direct route provided by United. Interestingly, on a recent visit to Hexham the bus station was exactly as I remembered it. One day I visited Allendale by bus on my own. It was a United Bristol single-decker, an MW I think. Why I should have wanted to visit Allendale I'll never know.

It was during the last mentioned holiday that Dad announced his redundancy as a shipyard engineer; he was clutching at straws when he took a job that delighted me and became a bus conductor with the Corporation. My delight was short lived, however, as I discovered I couldn't spend all my spare time riding round with him. In fact, I wasn't allowed to ride with him at all unless I happened to catch the bus he was working and even then I had to pay my fare. I learned more about bus types and could soon tell a Crossley from a Guy or a Daimler and that the rear-engined double-deckers were called 'Fleetlines'.

I've already said we had relations in the London area and, with four children about to leave school, my parents decided that employment prospects would be better for all of us 'down south' and when an advert appeared in the local paper, somebody wanting a council house swap from Ware in Hertfordshire to Sunderland. My parents replied and we moved south.

In the next chapter I'll tell you about the move, the language difficulties and London Transport buses.

OK (YUP 487) Leyland PD3/Roe, new to the operator in 1958 in West Auckland when in its twentieth year.

Hunter, Seaton Delaval 18 (ETY 912), a 1951 all-Leyland PD2 seen in Whitley Bay in 1970.

The move to Hertfordshire brought me into contact with buses with the smallest seating capacity in the London Transport fleet, although at that stage I had no idea we would share a workplace! GS33 in Loudwater village operating a journey on route 336A, the last route served by the GS class.

Chapter Two – The In-Between Years

In the last chapter I told you of my years in Sunderland. This time we look at my years in Hertfordshire. The way we moved was interesting; the pantechnicon van was a Bedford O type or something similar. It looked old even in 1964 and was hired from Street's of Hertford which, it turned out, was also a bus operator. It arrived the evening before the move with the Ware people's furniture in it, next morning that came out and ours went in. Dad was already in the south to receive it and the rest of us went to grandparents for the rest of the day. Mam, two sisters and myself then caught the overnight United coach to Hatfield (the Hertfordshire one) alighting at the Red Lion at about 5am. We then crossed the road to the railway station where a roaring fire welcomed us in the waiting room. The ticket clerk phoned a taxi for us and a wonderful Austin Princess, big, black and stately, turned up and whisked us off to our new home. Grandparents then brought the third sister by train at the weekend.

The first problem we had to overcome was the language; Sunderland has a very strong dialect (as does Barnsley to give a local example)., The people of Ware thought we were all foreigners as they struggled to understand us.

The local bus operator was London Transport in their green and cream Country Area livery. This seemed very boring after the variety in Sunderland. I soon realised that most of the double-deckers were classified RT, but some were RMC and wore two-tone green with the name Green Line. Most single-deckers were RF. Occasionally I would see a most unusual-looking single-decker called GS with protruding bonnet similar to the Jolly bus Bedfords.

I enrolled as a pupil at Ware Secondary Modern, where they once more tried (without success) to modernise me. Again I missed out on a bus to school as we lived about five minutes walk away but I would envy those arriving by Biss Bros, Street's, Cannon and other buses or coaches. Trips to Ware baths were by double-deck bus so I didn't mind swimming lessons. A visit to Whipsnade Zoo was by two RT type buses from Street's, I think.

Hertford was the nearest town of any significance to me; it had a bus station with a London Transport enquiry office from which I purchased a bus timetable for LT's North East Country Area. I discovered I could go to Harlow, where I found Eastern National buses, then Bishop's Stortford, more Eastern National and Premier Travel then back to Ware. In the opposite direction was Stevenage and Hitchin with United Counties buses and a firm called Birch running single-deckers between Rushden and Old Welwyn. From Hertford I could get to St Albans and Luton with Corporation buses in a dark red colour scheme and more United Counties. If I ventured as far as Hemel Hempstead Rover bus ran to Chesham and I tried their Bedfords a time or two. To the south of Ware the 310 ran to Waltham Cross and Enfield in LT's red bus territory.

Using a Green Rover ticket costing 3/- (15p) valid on all country buses but not Green Line, I once tried to circumnavigate London without any planning, probably not realising how big the Country Area was. Setting off at a leisurely 8am first to Hertford then St Albans, Uxbridge and Windsor where I decided I wouldn't make it all the way round and turned back, I then bought a full set of Country Area timetables and worked out a route starting about 6am to Harlow, then Epping from where a red RF on the 250 route took me to Romford. I had to pay on that. Then it was green buses all the way via Tilbury, crossing the Thames by ferry to Gravesend, thence Dartford, Sevenoaks, Westerham, Reigate, Leatherhead, Chertsey, Staines, Windsor, Uxbridge, St Albans and back to Ware on the last bus from Hertford. There were probably a few more places in between but after fifty years I can't remember them all. A new type to me was an RLH lowbridge Regent III between Chertsey and Staines on the 462.

One Hertford route I had to try was the 386, if for no other reason than to see how it worked. Basically the route was T shaped with Hertford and Ware at the south of the T, Standon at the north, Bishop's Stortford to the east, Stevenage and Hitchin west. On Tuesdays it ran Hertford – Hitchin, Thursdays Hertford – Bishop's Stortford and Saturdays Bishop's Stortford – Hitchin. A big bonus was that it was GS operated, my first experience of these funny little buses.

I would return to Sunderland to visit grandparents, usually unaccompanied. United coaches were always the way, occasionally travelling from Victoria but mostly from Hatfield. By this time the LS coaches had been replaced by MW or RE types. To me the latter represented the utmost in luxury with 45 seats in 36 feet of coach. When I visited South Shields the trolleybuses had gone and with London gone I assumed there were no more trolleys in Britain. One day I was riding round Northumberland by bus and in Whitley Bay I saw a very smart all Leyland PD2 belonging to Hunters of Seaton Delaval and caught it to North Shields., It was immaculate. I was saddened to see it some years later in a scrap yard. ETY 912 was new to Hunters in 1951.

Dad suggested I think about what I wanted to do when I left school, I didn't need to think, I'd known all my life I wanted to be a bus driver. I was most disappointed to find I'd have to wait 'til I was 21 years old for that, six years after leaving school. A conductor then, no it was eighteen years old for that. It would have to be an inspector, no only conductors became inspectors. Devastation! Was there no way I could work on the buses? Dad asked me who maintained the buses, I hadn't thought about that; why not apply for an apprenticeship was the advice. I duly cycled to LT's Hertford Garage and asked at the enquiry window. I was given an application form which I eagerly completed and sent off to Griffith House. A letter soon came back saying apprentices were only employed at the works, either Chiswick or Aldenham but a Garage Trainee scheme was carried out at local garages.There were no vacancies at Hertford but they would inform me if one became available.

Dad suggested I tried lorry operators for a garage job and I was successful with Warecrete Products who operated two-stroke Commers on breeze block distribution and Thames Traders on ready-mix. Some of the latter were six-wheelers converted by All Wheel Drive (AWD who later bought the Bedford production rights). Four-wheel Traders had the 4D engine whilst six-wheelers used the 6D, all had a 4D 'donkey engine' to drive the mixing drum. I was allocated to a fitter, Ivan, who maintained the Commers. I was fascinated by the workings of this three-cylinder opposed piston engine, more so when we stripped down and rebuilt one, starting it up without exhaust manifold and watching the pistons going up and down (well side to side actually). I came to really appreciate this type of engine and their sound when properly silenced. I was less impressed with the Traders; somehow they just weren't as exciting.On cold mornings one driver would pull the starting lever in the cab whilst another wound it up with the starting handle. Ivan left after a few months and I wasn't allocated to another. I was shown how to mend punctures, and there were plenty. At 15 years old the 900 x 20 wheels and tyres seemed bigger than me but I enjoyed fixing them, chucking them about to get tyres off and on the wheels, removing and refitting wheels to the vehicles.

I cycled to and from work, twice daily as I went home for dinner. We lived at the top of a steep hill and my bike had no gears. I would stand up on the pedals to get up the hill and snapped the chain many times. I got so dirty at work that Mam said I jumped in a bath of old oil as soon as I got there.

The best Christmas present I've ever had came in 1965 when a letter arrived from London Transport saying if I still wanted a job at Hertford I should to report to Griffith House, Marylebone Road, at a particular time and day. If I still wanted? Of course I still wanted! I must have been keen as I turned up a day early! I was interviewed, given amedical and advised to put in my notice at Warecrete and start at Hertford early next year.

Chapter Three – London Transport

In January 1966 I started what would be a lifetime in the bus industry. On my first morning at Hertford I reported to the Garage Engineer, a Mr Penny. People in authority didn't have first names in those days, they were all Mr. I was introduced to the two storemen I was to work with in the stores 'til my 16th birthday. The Storemen were 'green card' workers, on light duties due to ill health or whatever. One of them, Tom Dennis, was a former bus mechanic and he showed me round the garage pointing out the different bus types, took me into the workshop during the dinner time shut down and showed me the underside of buses so that I could see the differences between types.

I was loaned a staff pass with 'BEARER ON DUTY' stamped where the name should be and 'BEARER' stamped where the signature should be. Mr Penny told me to use it until my own pass arrived. Conductors accepted this without question but one day an inspector queried it, "What was I doing on duty out of uniform and on a Saturday afternoon?" I was still only 15 at the time and very embarrassed as the bus was full. I explained that I had just started as a Garage Trainee and he reluctantly accepted that. When my own pass arrived it was valid on all Country Area green buses, all Central Area red buses and the Underground and I made full use of it.

The staff pass was not valid on Green Line as this was considered a coach service. The vehicles were known as coaches but were really just buses with deeper seats, luggage racks and platform doors (on the Routemasters). They were crewed by long service staff and worked cross London routes, in our case the 715 Hertford to Guildford (RMC) and 715A Hertford to London Oxford Circus (RCL).

Soon after I had settled in at Hertford Ivan knocked at our door and asked for Jim. Which one he was asked, Granddad was living with us by then and three of us had the same name. Ivan had called to see if I wanted to continue my training with him as he had persuaded his new employer to take me on. He was thanked very graciously but, no, I now had the job I'd always wanted, well almost.

I quickly learned that London Transport didn't exist, it was 'The Board'. Double-deckers were 'decker s' and single-deckers were 'saloons' and everything was coded or abbreviated, bus types, garages, staff positions, everything; Hertford Garage was HG, I was a GT (Garage Trainee), Bus Mechanics were BMs, engines were EN etc. I found out that RT, RF, RMC and RCL types were all built by AEC. RTs were Regent III, RF Regal IV, RMC Routemaster Coach, RCL a longer RMC, GS stood for Guy Special, built by Guy Motors. I was told that the GSs had 'crash' gearboxes, not only that but the gears were the opposite way round in the box to most other types. There was one red bus based at HG; RTW 495, a Leyland-built RT type, was eight foot wide whereas the other RT, RF and GS were 7' 6" wide. The RTW, used for driver training, was known as the 'red learner'.

Some red RTL 'deckers were knocking about, RT Leyland apparently, as The Board was in the process of selling large numbers of Leyland 'deckers to the Ccylon Transport Board and each would receive a complete set of overhauled chassis units. Hertford dealt with a lot of this work, carried out on overtime by BMs who then drove the buses to the docks for export. Not all of the buses reached Ceylon though as RTL 1028 picked an argument with a dockside crane and suffered severe roof damage and RTL 593 attacked a low bridge resulting in the loss of its complete roof. Both buses returned to HG where units were transferred to other vehicles.

I attended East Herts College on day release and night school studying for City & Guilds in Motor Vehicle Mechanics, I achieved this with credit but by the time I wanted to continue on a Technician's course I was out of my training and had great difficulty persuading my employer to allow me time off. By the time they agreed I had missed the first term, I started after Christmas but they'd switched to metric by then and I'd missed the introduction to this. I failed the Technician exam miserably and have never got to grips with metrification. I have to admit to knowing two metric measurements though; the thou and the hundredweight.

Hertford carried out steam cleaning and repaints on buses belonging to Harlow, Hatfield and Stevenage garages and one day a Hatfield Routemaster arrived bearing bonnet number RMC 4 (LT never referred to fleet numbers, they were always bonnet numbers), I thought it had come to have the rest of the numbers added as all RMC's were in the 14xx or 15xx series. Tom Dennis explained this was an experimental Routemaster built by Leyland and ECW and was indeed RMC 4.

An unusual job carried out by the coachbuilders, as the body men were known, and painters was the conversion of two former BEA one and a half deck coaches into uniform distribution units. Their interiors were removed and replaced with shelving, a counter and changing rooms. They were then painted grey and signwritten.

I knew that registration letters were issued by local authorities and the last two letters represented the town of issue, all our RT's wore registrations between HLW and OLD but Biss Bros were running what was definitely an RT registered BDJ xxx. I queried this with Tom and he said it must be an STL; I knew it wasn't. It took quite a few years to find out that St Helens Corporation had some buses built to RT specification and this was one of those.

Overhaul

One day a brand new-looking RT came into HG. Tom took me to peruse this apparition, RTs hadn't been built for at least eleven years by then but here was a brand new one. Tom then explained LT's overhaul system where each bus consisted of three parts, body, chassis and identity and all three were interchangeable.

Every few years each bus was taken into Aldenham works, its body and chassis separated and each part overhauled including new flooring, seats, lining panels, the lot, then a complete repaint inside and out. It really did look like a new bus. He explained that neither the body nor chassis would have come from the bus that entered the works with that number as a works float system was employed. This involved a number of vehicles permanently de-licenced whose body and chassis were used on the road bearing identities of licenced buses, those in the works then assumed the identity of the de-licenced ones. So when RT 4747 (OLD 533) left Hertford and entered Aldenham the registration, bonnet, chassis numbers and licence discs would have been transferred to a similar vehicle that was ready to return to its garage bearing the identity of RT 4747 (OLD 533).

All this was carried out with Ministry approval as was the system where each bus was serviced once a month on a rota basis lasting eighteen months, Ministry inspections took place at the eighteenth month. So for LT an annual inspection occurred every eighteen months. The Ministry man ran a diesel Morris Oxford car and this was always parked next to the fuel pumps, somehow we never had a failure.

Occasionally buses would appear at HG on trade plates and full of gauges; they were on test from Chiswick works and included a very unusual Routemaster, bonnet No (even though it didn't have a bonnet) FRM1, this remains unique as the only rear-engined Routemaster.

At the age of sixteen I was at last let loose underneath buses. For the uninitiated that's where most bus maintenance takes place. I was really pleased to be getting my hands dirty again and learning to maintain and service RTs, RFs and RMCs, the RCLs had been replaced by RFs by then. I don't remember dealing with any the of the GS class. It wasn't just hands that got dirty though, at certain rota inspections the bus floor would be treated with something like creosote (I wish I could remember its name!). One painter, Bill Splevins, would apply so much it would drip through the floor traps onto those below.

Photography

On one of my visits 'home' I discovered a book, British Bus Fleets No 10 Northern, published in January 1967., I purchased same for the 5/- (25p) cover price. It gave details of all the major fleets in the Northern Traffic Area and listed another 21 books in the same series; I eventually bought all of these. It also advertised 'Buses Illustrated' magazine which I ordered monthly from my local newsagents.

A workmate, Bill Ruggles, suggested I start photographing buses and another, Cyril Foster, loaned me a camera. After a trial roll with black and white print film I bought my own camera, a Cosmic 35. Cyril suggested I use slide film saying that once a projector and screen had been purchased slide film would work out cheaper. I took his advice and took only slides for the next 44 years before going digital and I'm still using the screen!

Driving

From receiving my first pay packet I started saving to buy a car, I simply wanted to drive. Three-wheelers could be driven from the age of sixteen and as soon as I thought I had saved enough I started buying 'Exchange & Mart' looking for something suitable. What I bought was a 1960 Isetta bubble car, registered 367 JUR. Most lads made do with a motorbike or a scooter but not Jim; it had to be a car. Dad had only passed his driving test two years previously so he was able to teach me but recommended a professional lesson just before my test, which cost me 17/6d, (87½) it would have been £1 but I had to use my own car. This was the only driving lesson I ever paid for. I failed the test for not applying the handbrake at a major road junction but passed at the second attempt without further instruction and obtained a licence to drive a tricycle, a moped and a vehicle controlled by a pedestrian.

So at the age of 16 I was driving and owned my own car. The bubble car proved to be quite troublesome and I soon tired of it. I advertised the car for sale but on the day the advert appeared the head gasket blew, filling the car with exhaust smoke. To remove the head the engine had to come out and this was what greeted my first potential buyer. Fortunately, he had a phone number and I was able to contact him when repairs were completed. I fitted a new gasket and refitted the engine then he came back and bought the car.

Knowing that when I reached 18 years old the Board would train me to drive I bought a 1961 Reliant three-wheeler, a Regal Mark VI registered 9943 MY. The side valve engine was derived from the Austin 7 with thermo syphon cooling and no water pump or thermostat. This was more reliable and I even drove it to Sunderland and back, some 500 miles round trip, with my youngest sister on board. I was 17 by then.

On reaching eighteen I was put into the driving school with Hertford's driving instructor, Ted Barnes, in an Austin LD van with diesel engine and 'crash' gearbox, bonnet No 1119AS, registered WYL 716. Two weeks were allocated and I really enjoyed them. Semaphore indicators were controlled by a switch on the dash and Ted suggested I ignore them and use only hand signals, "you'll only forget to switch them off" was the advice, but I was used to such a switch and switched it on and off without thinking. Hand signals still had to be used though.

The whole thing vibrated fiercely on tick over and would shake my watch around my wrist if I held it on the handbrake. We would visit Chiswick almost daily as this was the driving school HQ. Here I would watch skid pan training where the instructor would pull the bus handbrake on and steer to the right, the bus would then swerve and skid sideways 'til it ran out of smooth, wet tarmac and the wheels hit concrete. The wheels would stop and the rest keep going, sideways! It would then rock vigorously from side to side, very frightening to watch let alone sample. The trainee was then taught to control the skid and the bus would pull up straight on subsequent trips round.

Come to my test day, Ted stayed at Chiswick while I went out with the examiner. I was asked to read a registration number from the cab as the engine ticked over and the whole van shook. He passed me on this section but as we pulled away I noticed the number was nothing like I'd said! This was at the time we were converting to continental road signs. Both were displayed on a wall and I was tested on both. The examiner, in all his gold braid, would point a stick at various signs and the answer had to be snapped back to him; "no right turn sir!", "30mph sir!" or whatever. I'm pleased to say I passed the test.

RTL 593 in Hertford garage having attacked a low bridge in Bow when on its way to London Docks for export to Ceylon, obviously the bridge won the argument.

Author at the wheel of his Isetta bubble car.

1119AS Austin LD van in Hertford garage for my driving instruction.

London Transport RT 3605 (MLL 915) AEC Regent 3RT/Weymann in Green Line livery in Hertford Garage in 1969. The trolleybus traction poles in the background were re-cycled as lamp-posts.

Green Line RF modernised, on Hertford garage forecourt.

On the last day of Reading's trolleybuses, this was the scene in Mill Lane on the afternoon of 3rd November 1968. *(Colin Enticknap, copyright British Trolleybus Society)*

Reading 181 at the Roath depot of Cardiff Transport on 26th June 1969. The similarity in liveries of Cardiff and Reading Corporations can be clearly seen. *(FR Whitehead)*

Chapter Four – London Country

As I said at the beginning of this book, notes are not necessarily in date order and are from memory so they might not be exactly correct.

Mr Penny retired and was replaced by Bill Daly from Leyton who insisted on being called Bill. When he appeared without a tie one day somebody commented "no tie and call me Bill, he'll get no respect like that!"

I became a Bus Mechanic when I reached eighteen and shift cover was beckoning; first on nights, only two BMs worked nights with a small team of cleaners or General Hands (GH) in LT terms. I would cover for either of these grades and soon found I disliked working nights, it just seemed wrong. It did have some advantages though as I could go out and photograph weekday only buses. Next was 'running shift', earlies and lates. I got to like this as rest days were arranged in groups of three.

Time off

I mentioned earlier that dad ran an A35 van, appropriately registered BMC 359A, and when he came to dispose of it Bill Ruggles suggested I buy it and use it as a motor caravan, a bit small you might think but with the passenger seat removed and the space built up with a home-made table I could have a full length bed. Thus I was able to get about the country for only the cost of petrol.

Through British Bus Fleet handbooks I discovered that trolleybuses survived in Reading and took myself off to find them. I boarded a six-wheeler and the compressor was running, then it cut out and I thought he'd stalled the engine 'til it pulled away in silence. I'd forgotten how quiet they were! All the trolleys carried notices to the effect that their demise was looming and the last day was to be in about two weeks time, actually on the 3rd of November 1968.

Being my Sunday off I returned to Reading to witness the proceedings. Hundreds of enthusiasts attended; some with preserved buses and a carnival atmosphere prevailed. I discovered that five other trolleybus systems survived and joined the Reading Transport Society (RTS) as they seemed to have a lot to do with trolleybuses. I soon made my way to Bournemouth, Bradford, Teesside and Walsall and joined a tour of the Cardiff system using a Bournemouth trolleybus and another with Reading 181. The latter was very similar-looking to the native vehicles except that platform doors were fitted and we picked up a driver on his way to work, he looked at the doors and asked "are they going to put doors on all our trolleys?"

In November 1969 I joined a tour that would eventually see a complete change of life for me. I'll leave you to ponder that one whilst I get on with my work story.

Breakdowns

The first breakdown I attended was RF 550 stuck in a flood at Hadham on the 350 route. Another BM drove the replacement bus and travelled back on it in service. I was left guarding the one in the water. Eventually a farmer offered to tow it out with a tractor, I phoned this back to HG and two BM's came out with an RT. RF 550 was now out of the water and the RT was attached to the front with a chain, the standard and only method of towing. It was decided not to use the starter motor but to slacken off the injectors and tow the bus in gear to clear the waterlogged engine then tighten the injectors and tow start. Yes you can tow start a preselector! RT and RF then drove home in convoy with me as passenger.

I assisted a BM, Tim Campkin, with a puncture one evening near Buntingford; it took two because the wheel had to be lifted into and out of the replacement bus. We stopped at a pub on the way back and Tim remarked "If beer keeps going up at this rate it'll soon be two bob a pint!" That's two shillings or 10p for younger readers.

The diff on an RF failed on a hill one evening and I attended with another bus and an RT to tow it home, except that the RT wouldn't pull away on the hill with the RF on the back. The RF was rolled backwards to a flat spot but the RT still wouldn't pull it. A lorry had to be summoned from Romford Garage but even this wasn't enough and a Matador recovery vehicle was called from I know not where within LT and the

RF was towed home in the early hours. My parents were very worried when I didn't return home at the usual time, no phones in those days.

The only GS I remember working on was GS 60, sold to Bickers of Coddenham in Suffolk. I changed the clutch plate on overtime and was admonished by Bill Daly for parking it on the garage forecourt for a picture.

London Country

London Transport hived off the Country Area to the National Bus Company in 1970 and we became London Country Bus Services Ltd (LCBS) using the fleetname London Country. A new livery soon appeared with Canary Yellow replacing Chiswick Cream as the relief on Lincoln Green. This brightened up the appearance of the buses enormously. Some buses still went to Aldenham for overhaul but some were prepared for recertification at garages. The average age of the fleet was about eighteen years and were mostly crew operated. A batch of AEC Merlin saloons (MB) had just been delivered to be followed by some AEC Swift saloons classified SM which had been ordered by the Board and entered service with Surrey registrations reflecting the new company's head office in Reigate. Some of these were delivered to HG but only for pre-service inspection and transfer to other garages.

New buses

A number of one man operated (OMO) buses came second hand from other NBC companies as well as some diverted orders. New OMO buses ordered by LCBS consisted of 90 AEC Reliance (RP) semi coaches in traditional Green Line livery and 90 Leyland Atlanteans (AN) which arrived in another new livery of a lighter shade of green, known locally as 'National Green' and Canary Yellow, nowhere near as smart as Lincoln Green in my mind. All carried Park Royal bodywork. Many of the RPs were collected by Hertford from Park Royal, where a set of trade plates meant freedom of the works, they were pre-serviced and delivered to their rightful garages.

Driving school

At the age of twenty one I was back in the driving school this time with an RT; well several RTs in fact as training lasted four weeks for established staff, only two weeks for new starters. Bullying is the only way to describe the attitude of the instructors who shouted and swore at trainees at every opportunity. On my first day we visited Chiswick, still used despite us now being detached from LT. The instructor announced he would drive back to our base at St Albans and he did so on the M1 motorway, using the third lane, still allowed to buses at the time, to overtake lorries. I could only imagine the lorry drivers' thoughts, not only being overtaken by a double-deck bus but one bearing 'L' plates! Country RTs had a diff ratio of 4&4/7ths:1 and could thus achieve 52 mph.

After a month I took and passed the same driving test as a service driver but didn't receive a PSV licence, these weren't issued to garage staff as buses could be driven on a car licence when not in service. One day type training followed on each of RF, RMC and MB. LCBS ran only two GSs, out of Garston (Watford) Garage, and I tried to persuade them I needed training on these but they wouldn't wear that.

On my first day back at Hertford I was sent with an RF coach, retained at LT's Riverside (Hammersmith) garage as a spare for Green Line breakdowns. Riverside had attended an RMC with transmission problems and substituted the RF, I had to return the RF and drive the RMC, on which they had topped up the flywheel, back to HG. In the centre lane of a one way system in Stoke Newington there was a very loud clatter from the engine which promptly stopped. A passing policeman told me oil was leaking from the engine (actually the flywheel that had parted company with the engine). "It's a good job it wasn't an hour later" commented the PC "it would have caused chaos with the rush hour traffic". I was there for two hours waiting for LT to rescue the coach.

RF 71 on a road test; note the revised position of the fleetname.

One of London Transport's SM class (EGN 449J) with the author. Bearing the London registration when delivered, it was re-registered in Surrey as EPD 441J before entering service.

London Country RP 80 (JPA 180K), an AEC Reliance with Park Royal body, in Green Line livery outside Hertford garage.

Stevenage bus station with all three of the Metro-Scania saloons purchased by Stevenage Development Corporation in view.

Better Buses for Stevenage

The new town of Stevenage decided it needed better buses and a 'Better Buses for Stevenage' experiment took place, at first using three Daimler Fleetlines of the XF class in 'Blue Arrow' livery on services linking housing estates directly with the industrial area but Stevenage Development Corporation wanted even better buses and a Leicester Metro Scania single-decker was displayed with a standard London Country SM. A new livery of yellow and blue was adopted for the single-deckers that replaced the XFs. The Corporation purchased three Metro Scania saloons, classified MS, to operate alongside SMs on the 'Superbus' services.

As I mentioned earlier, steam cleaning of buses from neighbouring garages took place at HG and when an MS came in from Stevenage I arranged to drive it back. I found myself looking for a gear lever on this, my first attempt at a vehicle with automatic transmission.

In line with most NBC companies, London Country started to receive Leyland National saloons. The first of these were for Superbus work at Stevenage and were delivered in all over yellow, the blue relief being applied at Hertford. The only such vehicle I had any dealings with was one I took from Hertford to Romford. I called at home for my tea on the way and parked it outside our house.

All change at Hertford

April 1972 saw the introduction of 12 ANs to the 310 route and seven RPs to the 715, all were one man operated. We worked through the night moving buses between garages as most of our serviceable RTs and all our RMCs had to go to new homes, for some reason our RMCs went to Grays garage and were replaced by similar vehicles from Hatfield. The RPs settled down nicely on the route to Guildford but the ANs proved very troublesome on the Enfield route. It was as well that a few conductors remained and a number of RTs were still licenced to cover for these troublesome buses. Incidentally, having driven many RPs from the bodybuilders we all had to have two hours type training on the vehicles. In practice this was just time paid without any instruction.

In the next chapter I'll tell you about the life-changing tour and my life after that.

Leyland National LN 4 (NPD 104L) in as delivered condition in Hertford garage, painted yellow for *Superbus* work, the blue relief was applied at Hertford garage. *(John Law)*

These two individuals, Les Flint and Don Penney, were regularly to be found at Sandtoft, where they are seen together in front of Doncaster Trolleybus 375. They were stalwarts of both DOLRS (Doncaster Omnibus & Light Railway Society) and the fledgling Sandtoft Transport Centre. The photograph was taken by Mike Dare, whose role in the establishment of the centre is legendary. *(MJC Dare, copyright British Trolleybus Society)*

Chapter Five – Away From Work

I mentioned previously that I joined a tour in 1969 that would, eventually, change my life. That tour was advertised in 'Trolleybus' the journal of the Reading Transport Society. It would visit Manchester for a film show by Howard Piltz and an overnight stay, then on to Bradford to see the new city centre wiring of the trolleybus overhead and Doncaster to see the new trolleybus museum. The vehicle used was an ex-South Wales AEC Regent V from Smith's of Reading, it reached Manchester without problem if a little slowly and was fuelled and garaged at a Manchester Corporation depot. Next morning all was not well in the engine department and the Corporation was called out when it broke down at the roadside. Fitters attended, changed the fuel filter and away we went, only to break down again. Apparently Manchester fuel contained an additive to keep the pipes clean and this bus had never had clean pipes, all the crud from the pipes blocked the filter, twice!

Bradford was reached and the wiring inspected before continuing to Doncaster then out into the countryside where the bus pulled up at the roadside behind an ex-Bradford RT. Our driver came round to the back platform, he was furious that an expected building was non-existent, "what's it to do with him" I thought, "He's only the driver". It turned out that he was Mike Dare, owner of this site that was to become Sandtoft Transport Centre, later the Trolleybus Museum at Sandtoft. We were advised to board the RT whilst Mike went off to see the builder. No 410 took the party to the nearby yard of Selwyn Motors where several trolleybuses were stored awaiting the new depot. Proprietor of Selwyn, Barry Dodd, has been a friend ever since.

Shortly after the tour a notice appeared in 'Trolleybus' asking for volunteers to help with the new museum. I thought that a working trolleybus museum would need a bus mechanic so next Easter I packed my tool box, drove to Sandtoft and offered my services. There was now a shed on site holding seven trolleybuses and the aforementioned RT. There wasn't much I could do as there was no means of moving the vehicles but I met some very keen volunteers and enjoyed myself enough to return a few months later. By then traction poles were being planted and work was progressing. I discovered the Doncaster members were very friendly and my visits became more frequent. As I said earlier, I had bought an A35 van and had used it to sleep in on holidays all over Britain so Sandtoft was no problem. By now I had progressed to an A60 van, ELB 441C, much roomier but a lot more thirsty.

On one of my early visits I came across a marvellous man called Les Flint who always spoke very slowly and deliberately in a strong West Riding dialect. On hearing that I was to sleep in my van Les said "you can't sleep in your van, come and stay at our house." I politely declined saying I was used to sleeping in my van. "Well come and have your tea then, I'll tell t'missus you're coming". Les and Jean became very good friends of mine even going on holiday with them. Sadly, Les passed away in 1983 as did t'missus who was in a care home until 2016.

I found the rest of the Doncaster contingent at Sandtoft were all members of the Doncaster Omnibus & Light Railway Society (DOLRS for short) of which Les Flint was Chairman. I would join them in a pub after a day building the Museum where the main task was planting traction poles to support the trolleybus overhead. This was done entirely by hand as the only tools we had were an auger and an ex-Huddersfield poling crane and even these were hand wound. Les was in charge of this operation. There were no facilities on site so Thermos flasks and sandwiches were the norm although Jean Flint would bring a Primus stove and kettle and, sometimes, soup to keep the workers fed and watered whilst their Alsatian dog, Timba, would keep 'his flock' in check by nipping bottoms where he deemed it necessary.

When enough poles were in place the first span wire was erected using an ex-Bradford Karrier tower wagon. Now it was beginning to look like a trolleybus circuit but somebody forgot to lower the jib before towing the pole crane under the wire. There was a loud twang and said wire fell to the ground. Les stood back and proclaimed "I want to f**t"! The wire was hurriedly re-assembled before we all left site that day.

An AEC 9.6 engine coupled to a trolleybus traction motor powered the overhead. The engine would be racing at full throttle until the trolley took power then full load was applied and the engine nearly stalled. This was cruelty to diesel engines in my mind! We knocked out two AEC and a Gardner engine in this manner then substituted a Cummins, this proved too powerful and burnt out the traction motor and compressor on Maidstone 72. An automatic throttle advance system was devised and proved much more satisfactory but the best thing for me was when we were connected to the mains.

My visits to Sandtoft became more and more frequent and returning to Hertfordshire more of a pain. In the winter of 1972/3 I decided I'd had enough of the south and moved to live in Doncaster, more about the move later. At the Sandtoft AGM in March 1973 I was elected to the Committee in the position of Site Co-ordinator. Soon afterwards a workshop was envisaged and I was asked to take charge of that before it was even built. In 1988 I joined the board of Directors and four years later became Managing Director, not bad going for a simple bus mechanic. After 13 years I retired from the Board but remained in charge of the workshop in the role of Superintendent. I've given up the workshop several times but it always comes back to me. Don't get carried away thinking Sandtoft's workshop is anything special, it only holds one bus.

Doncaster Omnibus and Light Railway Society.

Membership of this society was by invitation only and soon after my move north Les announced that I was now a DOLRS member.

In June 1973 the Society acquired two buses on permanent loan from Doncaster Corporation, No 22, MDT 222, a 1953 AEC Regal III/ Roe and No 94, EDT 703, a 1947 Leyland PD2 with a 1955 Roe body that was originally carried on trolleybus No 393 and transferred to 94 in 1963. 22 had been adopted by the Society and used for trips and excursions for some years whilst still in service, 94 had operated over one million miles in service and the Corporation wanted to see it preserved. These joined 1945 Karrier W/ Roe (1955) trolleybus No 375, CDT 636, on permanent loan from the Corporation. 22 soon joined 375 at Sandtoft whilst 94 stayed at the Corporation depot a while longer.

Only Les drove 22 and on one rally the dog was at the opposite side of the field. We were all on the bus and ready to leave when Les bellowed from the cab, "Timba, will you come here", dog came bounding over and screeched to a halt by the cab door, "no not in t'cab, in t'bus" Les retorted, Timba went round to the passenger door and boarded the bus.

Another early rally attended with 22 was at Dunbar. Les drove of course, and we spent all day Saturday getting there. About six of us slept in the bus including Jean and Timba. We did the road run on Sunday and Les drove back that evening.

94 has been much more work-shy, I drove it on the East Coast Run in 1974; Hull and Bridlington are a long way from Sandtoft at 30mph. The engine was past its best and a PD3 was purchased from Yorkshire Traction, T2 HCD 367E, an ex-Southdown 'Queen Mary.' After conversion from compressor to exhauster and mechanical to vacuum governor fuel pump the engine was fitted to 94. It only took 25 years to carry out the transplant since when it has seen only spasmodic rallying seasons.

We heard that an ex-Doncaster bus was for sale at Plumtree in Nottinghamshire and a number of DOLRS members formed a group to save this experimental 8' wide AEC Regent III/ Roe that had been No 122, KDT 393. The DOLRS 122 Group soon found there wasn't time to restore a bus at the same time as build a Museum and the bus passed to Tony Peart who restored it to a very high standard.

More permanent loans

Another vehicle joined the 'fleet' in 1979, ex-Doncaster 33, 433 MDT, a Roe-bodied Leyland Tiger Cub new in 1963. South Yorkshire PTE, as successor to Doncaster Corporation, offered the bus on the same "permanent loan" basis as the other three vehicles. This would be maintained by a member at no cost to the Society, how could we refuse? Two years later the PTE offered a further vehicle in the shape of ex-Doncaster 206, KDT 206D, a Daimler CVG6 again with Roe body. Again a sponsor was found and it would cost the Society nothing. Finally, for vehicle additions, a DOLRS member offered to donate to the Society Doncaster 112, GDT 421, a 1949 Daimler CVD6 with Roe lowbridge body. This had been partly restored and the donor would cover its storage fees.

Incidentally, when I tried to apply for a grant to restore our trolleybus I was asked if we owned the item, I replied it was on permanent loan. "You can't have a grant for anything on loan" I was told. "But it's

This view of the runway at Sandtoft taken in 1969 gives some idea of the undeveloped state of the site at the time. *(DG Chick)*

Another view of the site in 1969 with Doncaster 94 the lone vehicle in view. *(MJC Dare, copyright British Trolleybus Society)*

During the visit to Sandtoft described in the text, Smiths Regent V (NCY 451) also paid a visit to the Westgate Chapel owned by Mike Dare. Derby 172 may just be identified inside the premises. *(MJC Dare)*

Doncaster trolleybus 375, which was to be the last trolleybus to operate in the town and which was presented to DOLRS, is seen in St Sepulchre Gate about to depart on the Racecourse Circular. The buildings in the background have long since disappeared under the town centre shopping complex, originally called the Arndale Centre. *(Tony Belton)*

permanent loan, and we've had it 40 years". "You'll have to get the owner to sign it over". Who did own it? Doncaster Corporation had long since gone and the PTE had ceased to operate buses. A phone call to a contact at First bus confirmed none of our buses were on their books, "but we'll sign them over if you want us to" so First bus very kindly gave away five buses they didn't own! Then the grant application failed, but at least we now own all the vehicles in our care.

In the next chapter I'll return to my work in the bus industry.

Another view of Doncaster trolleybus 375 shows the outer terminus of the same service, with the Racecourse buildings in the background. *(Tony Belton)*

In June 1973 Doncaster Corporation placed two motorbuses on permanent loan to the Doncaster Omnibus and Light Rail Society, one of which was this Leyland PD2 which had been new in November 1947 and which was fitted with the 1955 trolleybus body previously carried on No 393 and fitted to the Leyland in 1963. The ex-trolleybus Roe bodies fitted to the Leyland chassis were all previously carried by former Mexborough vehicles which, being single deck, were 27 feet long hence the butchery to the front of the vehicles to allow the bodies to fit 26-foot chassis.

This Daimler CVG6, No 204, KDT 204D, with forward-entrance Roe body seating 72, was new to the Corporation in May 1966.

Chapter Six – The Move To Doncaster

By December 1972 I still hadn't settled in the south and, having made many friends in Doncaster, I applied to Doncaster Corporation for a fitter's job. They didn't need fitters at the time but were desperate for drivers and offered to train me to PSV standard if I would work as a driver until a garage vacancy occurred.

Free tuition

One Monday I attended the depot at Leicester Avenue for an interview and driving assessment. The bus used was No 193, a Roe-bodied Leyland PD3 front loader whose door valve was directly above first gear position. I had been taught by LT to ignore first and set off in second but thought I'd better do the job right on my assessment. Every time I engaged first I wrapped my knuckles on the door valve and ended up dripping blood everywhere. My PSV test appointment came soon after and I was given one day's free tuition in 188, 388 KDT, a Leyland PD2 with Roe body transferred from a trolleybus. This tuition was absolutely free as they didn't pay me and I didn't pay them. More bullying in the driving school. Again I thought I ought to set off in first gear but was shouted at and told to use second. When it came to a hill-start I engaged first and the instructor, Jimmy Johnson, bellowed "told you before we don't use bottom, gerrit in t'second!" It was necessary to pull up at a bus stop with the open rear platform next to the stop post. Jimmy had pushed a cigarette packet into the hedge at the stop used for this exercise and if your cab was level with this your platform was on the stop! London Transport had taught me to reverse round right hand corners by opening the cab door and leaning out, when I tried this in Doncaster Jimmy shouted " where do you think you're going, get back in t'cab!" reversing had to be done using mirrors. I passed the test next day.

Number 22

On Monday 22nd of January 1973 I started work with Doncaster Corporation; I was 22 years old and rented a flat at 22, Windsor Road. At the time DOLRS was in the process of acquiring AEC Regal III No 22, from the Corporation so 22 was my lucky number.

The job I always wanted

On my first day I was issued with a uniform and, with a few other new starters, set out route learning using a Seddon saloon with a spare driver at the wheel. Now I knew the main roads into and out of Doncaster but not the side roads or the names of districts and housing estates. Our trainer, Dave, delighted in taking short cuts, saying "we don't actually use this road but use the one we're just crossing". Dave was really pleased to have crammed three days route learning into two days but I ended up more confused than when I started. He asked if anybody was unsure of any route, one said Arksey, another said Woodlands and they were told to catch a bus and learn the route. "What about you, Jim?" he asked and I answered "all of them", "don't worry, you'll soon pick it up" was the reply.

Dave mentioned the Daimlers with preselector gearboxes. "You've all driven preselectors before haven't you?" he asked and all said they had, one said "we called then GCP's in the army" GCP standing for Gear Change Pedal so he obviously knew about them but I doubted the others had had any experience of this type of transmission. I had of course with RT's and RF's.

Wednesday 24th of January would have been my first day on the road but my badge hadn't arrived by then and this was a legal necessity for service driving, so I was sat spare in the canteen on Duke Street in the town centre. In the afternoon I was sent to depot to collect bus 144 for schools, and I was told to look after it as it was going into a museum when it came out of service, I knew that already but they didn't know I knew! My badge, No BB 66801, arrived that day and next day I was out on service on the Castle Hills route with a Daimler CVG6 front-loader 'decker, crew operated of course. This route was normally operated with Leylands and I was glad to have an air operated pre-selector instead.

Once the driver shortage had been overcome a lot of crews were spare in the canteen. One tea time a tannoy message told all spares to report to the Intake stand on Duke Street. Bus 94 wouldn't start and we had to push-start it full of passengers! 94 received a new set of batteries before it passed into preservation. Occasionally spare crews would be given a one-man duty with a one-man bus. This was hard work as passengers always wanted to pay the driver and took a lot of persuasion to sit down without paying. As crews now waited on Duke Street take their bus over, one summer's day a young woman in a mini-skirt walked past, she had a dog on a lead and one conductor remarked to her "Good afternoon madam, lovely pair of legs" she smiled at him then he added "On the dog"!

Converts

The Daimler CVG6s with former trolleybus bodies were known to the crews as 'converts'. I often wondered if they knew what they had been converted to or from. They were 'trolley Daimlers' to DOLRS members. They had spring operated pre-selector gearboxes and drivers soon learned to respect these. If the floor wasn't hit when engaging a gear the pedal would fly up under pressure and push the drivers leg into a seat winding handle. The only way to return it was to use both feet on the pedal and heave on the steering wheel, with the bus still in motion of course. This only happened once to each driver. Hills are hard to come by in Doncaster but there are some minor ones, with a Daimler the engine note changed and the bus continued at the same speed.

One-man-operation

After a few months I was put into the conductor's school for one-man (OMO) training. We spent about three days sitting at a long table asking the one opposite for "two and a half and a dog to somewhere please", looking up the fare in the fare book, issuing tickets from the Ultimate ticket machine, telling them the amount, taking money and giving change. Then we swapped places. There was also filling in waybills and changing ticket rolls on the five bank machine. Fares were very simple as the normal maximum was 4p except Edlington which was joint with East Midland Motor Services and cost 7p. Sheffield was another matter but that route was worked by crews on the 'Sheffield Sheet' certainly not by new starters. About a month after this training I hadn't done any one-manning and was booked on an OMO duty. I told the duty inspector I thought I might have forgotten some of the procedures. At the same time my conductor said he'd passed his driving test but hadn't driven so the inspector told us to swap jobs. I wasn't licenced for conducting but we swapped jobs for a few trips one Sunday on the Beckett Road route.

My first day's OMO was on Race Course route, a twenty minute round trip. After my meal break I was on Hyde Park, the same circular route but running in the opposite direction. Seddon RU's were used and the first thing I learned about these was that they wouldn't pull up in a straight line; they would pull to left on some brake applications and to right on others, more about that later. Centre doors were controlled by the gear lever and this meant pulling out two knobs, intended to need both hands but with a bit of fancy finger work one hand could be used. It was usual practice to open the middle doors as the bus was nearly at a standstill but on one occasion I managed to take first gear instead of opening the doors, the bus took a nose dive and a passenger came flying to the front. I merely said to him "middle door off, please!"

On Hexthorpe route passengers would ask for "Flats, please". I asked many people where the flats were as I'd never seen any and they all told me the same, at the terminus. The reason I hadn't seen any flats was that it was the name of the park.

I mentioned Les Flint earlier and he was a night foreman at Leicester Avenue depot. We would often chat at the beginning of my day (early) shift or at end of an afters (late) shift. One morning I had a run to do from Edlington. My bus was No 65 a Seddon, and I forgot the time as I chatted to Les. I realised my lateness, jumped in the bus and drove off. It was practice then to always show the outer destination only. No 65 was showing Depot and, as Edlington buses didn't pick up in Balby, I thought it would do in view of my lateness. I picked up in Edlington but passengers were putting out their hands on Balby Road. I drove past them until I had to drop off and a passenger tried to board. I explained this was an Edlington bus and didn't pick up at that stop. "Says Balby on t'front" complained one passenger. I opened the box and she was right. Then I looked at the bus number and it was 68, Les realised my mistake and told Control he'd told me to take that one.

It took twelve minutes to walk from home to depot and I would leave home twelve minutes before I was booked on, occasionally a spare driver would be sent to prepare my bus because they thought I wouldn't turn up. At the end of the day drivers stayed with their bus whilst it was fuelled then drove it through the wash and parked it. We would be asked on the pumps, "Is it alright?" we dreaded saying "yes" as the next instruction would be "Put it in t'hangar". A First World War aircraft hangar remained in the back yard and buses had to be reversed into it.

Another 22

In April and May 1973 DCT purchased three Seddon Pennine 4 midibuses numbered 22-24, TDT 622-4L. They were for a new route to West Bessacarr and worked by specially selected drivers. DOLRS Bus Club meetings were held at Les and Jean's house and Les announced "Little 22's got black teeth!"; the radiator grille was painted black. For the 1973 Sandtoft Gathering I was nominated to take little 22, following Les Flint in the real 22. I soon found the brakes grabbed, just gentle pressure resulted in a very rapid deceleration. Naturally I reported this but later found it was the norm as these 26 seater buses had the same air braking system as full size buses. One day one of the regular drivers, Bill Hicks, took No 24 into the depot as the brakes were grabbing. The fitter took it for a road test and Bill accompanied him. At the first brake application Bill was catapulted through the windscreen!

Last AEC

On Monday 2nd July 1973 the first of fifteen new Roe-bodied Daimler Fleetlines entered service, replacing the last of the exposed radiator AEC Regent V's. Les Flint persuaded the Corporation that the Regents would be needed on Sunday 1st and to prove this he booked most of them out on service. He saved No 157 so that we could have a play with it on a farewell tour. No 144 entered preservation with Don Penney after DCT fitted a reconditioned engine and repainted it for him.

The next chapter will tell you about my time working in the depot.

All the 2s again! Seddon Minibus No 22, new in April 1973, is specially posed at Leicester Avenue depot next to AEC Regal No 22, which had been withdrawn the previous October and presented to the Doncaster Omnibus and Light Railway Society on permanent loan.

Doncaster 179, a Daimler CV6/30 with Roe H40/32F body, was one of a group of buses introduced in December 1963 to replace the town's last trolleybuses.

Doncaster took delivery of its first rear-engined double-deckers in 1967, Daimler Fleetlines with Roe bodies, and No 219 is from a similar batch delivered in 1970. Seen in original livery on Duke Street in the town centre.

Despite being in charge of one of the Doncaster Seddons, which proved to be challenging from a maintenance point of view, I still managed a smile in this photo at the Wheatley Hills terminus.

Regent V No 157 was the last of its type in service, on 1 July 1973, and is seen here in Green Boulevard being overtaken by Fleetline No 219, now bearing the purple stripe colour scheme, on the Cantley Estate service.

Doncaster operated an ex-RAF AEC Matador recovery vehicle, the body having been rebuilt by the Corporation. It is seen here coming to the aid of Leyland Royal Tiger Cub No 55 (now in preservation) at Arksey terminus.

Amongst the other ancillary vehicles operated by the Corporation, this Austin FGK 2-ton lorry, No 6 (XDT 679G) was purchased in December 1968. (despite Les's comment in his book this is an FG).

Chapter Seven – Into The Depot

Eventually a vacancy occurred in the depot and I moved 'inside' in October 1973 initially in the ancillary shop working on vehicles belonging to other departments of the Corporation, mainly ambulances but including the Mayoral Daimler car, buses belonging to local schools and Transport Department vehicles other than buses, an Austin FG lorry, Ford Escort and Transit vans, an ex-Military AEC Matador recovery vehicle with cab built in the Corporation body shop and several cars. We had to drive the ambulances on trade plates as they were only licensed for qualified ambulance crews to drive. Once on a road test I approached road works with stop-go boards, when the man saw the ambulance approaching he stopped all the other traffic and waved me through! The vehicles were mostly Ford Transits but with a few Bedford CA's and one Morris LD. They decided to convert the LD into a major incident unit and we removed the bench seating, I acquired those seats and transported them to Sandtoft where they served the mess room for about 30 years. The school buses included Hayfield's Dennis Lance, Balby Carr's Leyland Royal Tiger and few Bedford SBs; I usually managed to road test them.

The steam cleaning bay was next to the ancillary shop and one day the man employed on this work, George Sanderson, entered our shop. He was black from head to foot; the only thing white was the cigarette sticking out of his mouth. He'd come in for a light but was unlucky as none of us smoked! On one occasion one of the four electric motors that worked the lift failed with a bus aloft, a perfectly serviceable bus was stuck there for a few days until the motor could be overhauled.

One incident much talked about at the time was when an apprentice tried to put a bubble car onto a pit. The back wheel dropped in and, with a front opening door, said apprentice couldn't get out. A group of fitters then lifted car out of the pit and carried it shoulder high round the depot with lad still in it!

South Yorkshire PTE

A celebration of Doncaster Corporation Transport took place on Sunday 31st March 1974; this involved DO&LRS touring all the current routes during the day using 188, the PD2, and all the former tram routes in the evening using Daimler CVG6 No 202. Another group was touring all three Municipalities using one bus from each running in convoy and we had arranged to meet them at Leicester Avenue depot. As we awaited their arrival outside the Corporation Fire Station, which was next to the depot, one of the firemen offered to move all the appliances out for us, an offer we couldn't refuse and we had a look at the fire station. "After all it's our last day with the Corporation as well" he commented.

On all fool's day 1974 South Yorkshire Passenger Transport Executive took over the assets of Doncaster, Rotherham and Sheffield Corporation Transport departments and the buses started to appear in a new livery of 'coffee and cream' but the coffee was so weak that it was difficult to see where this ended and cream started. Black lining was applied to distinguish the two but this must have been expensive to apply and gradually the 'coffee' shade was darkened. On Friday 30th March Doncaster 190, a PD3, appeared in service during the afternoon peak wearing the new livery. The fleet was renumbered by adding one thousand to the Corporation number but paint shop soon ran out of number 1s and some saloons appeared as 0xx. Only one Doncaster vehicle missed out on 'purplisation', No 96, a 1947 PD2 with body previously carried on an ex-Mexborough trolleybus chassis, was being converted to a breakdown vehicle at the time of take over and went from red and white to 'coffee and cream'. This must have been the only Mexborough trolleybus ever cut down for towing!

Work for the ancillary shop was much reduced at the time of take over and I moved onto the main bus fleet. I spent some time on the brake pits where trying to solve the Seddon's braking problems meant adjusting them on the road by applying full steering lock and winding the appropriate adjuster to achieve a straight line stop. Shaftesbury Avenue, a wide straight housing estate road near the depot, was covered in tyre marks due to all brake testing being carried out there using a Tapley decelerometer. Asbestos linings had to be riveted to the shoes and a leading edge applied using a bench grinder. I always say I should have died years ago, the amount of asbestos I've swallowed. At least I won't be cremated; I must be full of the stuff! Incidentally we never jacked buses up to adjust brakes; brakes were wound up to the full

Hayfield School operated a Dennis Lance registered NTE 823, seen in Stainforth.

Balby High School operated this Leyland Royal Tiger registered KWX 549. Picture taken in the depot yard after the ex-Severn's vehicle had been painted in the Transport Department paint shop.

The Dennis Fire Engine that was posed for a photograph during the tour to mark the demise of Doncaster County Borough Council on 31st March 1974.

On the same day, representatives of the three fleets that were to form South Yorkshire PTE from the following day met up in Leicester Avenue depot.

Leyland PD2 188, with a body from trolleybus 395, was also used on 31st March 1974 for a farewell tour of Doncaster Transport's routes. That to Burghwallis was probably as rural as any Doncaster corporation bus service could be. The vehicle is now in preservation following its use as a training bus. Along with many other drivers I passed my PSV test in this bus.

The new owners, the PTE, soon commenced repainting vehicles into its new corporate colours, which did not meet with general acclamation.

An early candidate for the new livery was former bus No. 96, which Doncaster Transport had been in the process of converting to a towing wagon and tree lopper.

Former Corporation, KDT 206D was offered by the PTE to DOLRS on the same basis as the previous Corporation 'permanent loans'.

The PTE experimented with a number of demonstrators in its early years, and a Volvo Ailsa, with Alexander body, (THS 273M) makes an appearance in Doncaster.

A Van Hool McArdle-bodied Atlantean was also operated and the PTE was subsequently to combine elements of both demonstrators by ordering 62 Ailsas with Van Hool McArdle bodies.

A few years before the PTE was formed, DCT decided to enter the Private Hire market, and chose the Ford chassis for its coaches. This R114 model had, for its time, rather exotic Moseley Continental Caetano bodywork.

No explanation is needed really for former DT 40, a Leyland Royal Tiger Cub, now showing PTE fleet number 1040, seen here in Leicester Avenue depot.

Turning across the A630 at Balby, Seddon RU 1065 replicates the manoeuvre carried out previously by trolleybuses for some 20 years.

Allocated to Doncaster by the PTE, 801 was one of six Daimler Fleetlines with ECW bodies which entered service in late 1974.

then slackened off 'til it was possible to rock the bus by pushing on the wheel. Diaphragm rubbers were changed annually, the only place I've known to this to be done. I learned that 'bedding in' the brakes often did more good than anything else; this involved applying the brake pedal whilst driving in gear and would be done after reline or to dry them out after steam cleaning.

Seddons

The Corporation must have thought they'd found a real bargain when they ordered Seddon RUs, with rear-mounted Gardner engines and Wilson gearboxes. The first batch had aluminium-framed Seddon Pennine bodies, the others Roe. Similar specifications to the Bristol RE/ECW but on those the gearbox was mounted forward of the back axle, on the RU the engine and gearbox were close coupled behind the axle and everything was crammed in together. The flywheels overheated and leaked requiring engine removal to fit new seals. This involved cutting the rear cross member and bolting a plate in to join it together again. Changing back springs necessitated using a long bar that bent and twisted across the chassis and came out of the opposite wheel arch. The nylon spring bushes wore badly and the pins became seized. Hitting the bar with a sledge hammer had little effect as the bends absorbed all the shock. Then the Pennine bodies started to flex above the middle door. They all lasted into PTE ownership but were withdrawn soon after. The depot floor was very slippery, especially when wet and once I touched the brake on a Seddon and slid into a pillar, of which there were plenty, knocking a mirror off in the process. I merely spoke nicely to the body shop foreman, Pete Michinson, and he replaced the mirror without any paperwork.

One day I caught the radio emergency button by mistake. The foreman, who was in the bus with me, picked up the microphone and said "Sorry, accident. Over" to which Control asked "What kind of accident, do you need an ambulance? Over" Another time I took a bus out on road test and the inspector's van came chasing after me, apparently the radio was faulty and blocking the entire system, I had to return to depot and get an electrician to sort it out.

Demonstrators

The PTE sampled a few demonstrators in its early years including two Ford A series midibuses, a Ford R1014, two Atlanteans, one a Leeds bus with Leyland G2 automatic transmission, the other an Irish bus with Van Hool McArdle body. THS 273M was an Ailsa that disgraced itself by breaking down whilst driver training prior to entering service and spent a week parked in depot awaiting parts. It must have been successful as a batch of 62 Ailsas was purchased; all had Van Hool McArdle bodywork which soon developed galloping rot. Ailsa's were assembled from Volvo parts including the small, turbocharged engine. The turbos soon developed a very distinctive scream and enthusiasts would 'go for a scream on an Ailsa'. Two battery powered electric buses were tried, a Seddon Midi and a large Seddon similar to the RU, both hired from Greater Manchester PTE.

The PTE introduced a time-related bonus scheme and it didn't take long for some people to find ways to increase their bonus. One cleaner found that instead of spraying engines with degreaser then washing it off he could spray all engines one day and wash them all off next day, he hadn't realised it wasn't the same buses in depot every day and those he'd sprayed would go out on service only to return booked off for fumes.

We were required to clock on and off and, at the end of the day, were supposed to stay in our respective workshops until a bell sounded but in practice all would be lurking in the nearest 'shop to the clock or hiding behind vans or buses parked nearby and would suddenly appear at the clock when the bell sounded.

I left the PTE in June 1975 and moved to work at Blue Line which I will tell you about next.

Another Leyland Atlantean that was examined was loaned from West Yorkshire PTE, their 6003 (UWT 603N) fitted with automatic transmission.

Before the fleet of Ailsas had been delivered, another experimental group of buses had entered service with the PTE, and all were based in Doncaster. Turning out of Duke Street, No 504 was one of a handful of Metro-Scania double-deckers. Like examples elsewhere in the country, the stay with their original owner was brief.

Chapter Eight – The Blue Line Years

In June 1975 I left the PTE and started as a fitter/driver with the independent operator, Blue Line. There were two companies in common management, S Morgan, trading as Blue Line running from two depots, and R Store t/a Reliance based in Stainforth. Buses were 'ours' or 'theirs' but we would work on either. I'll refer to both as Blue Line for simplicity. I was based at Armthorpe where a new workshop had been built, by far the best I've worked in. The only problem was that it was built behind Woodlea House, the Company office; there was just enough room to get a 36-foot coach in.

The Managing Director was John Wilson, who was known as 'Doggy' due to his father breeding dogs at the time of John's birth. Edgar Stones was chief mechanic, Colin Newton mechanic. Edgar was 65 years old and I was set on to replace him but he didn't retire, Colin was 45 and both had been there from school! Colin's wife, May, was a cleaner/conductress and her Uncle Hughie bus fueler and washer. There was a definite family feel to the company. Mr Theaker was the Company Secretary and would often come into the garage clutching a piece of paper. "Don't know what we're going to do" he would say. One day he'd had a letter from the West Riding Automobile Company announcing their intention to increase fares between Goole and Radcliffe to 21p, a journey time of ten minutes. They were asking us to do likewise on that common stretch of route. "I can't do that", said Mr Theaker, "We only charge 22p from Goole to Doncaster" about a 75 minute journey. I suggested he asked them to reduce their fares in line with ours.

I was introduced to some vehicle types new to me including Bedford VAL and the magnificent Guy Arab. There were Bedford VAS, VAM and SB5, Ford coach, Leyland PD3 and Daimler Fleetline, all of which I had encountered previously. My duties usually included school runs morning and afternoon with garage work in between. The main operating centre was at Stainforth but most engineering was carried out at Armthorpe where the allocation consisted of two Fleetlines, two PD3, one each of coach-bodied Bedford VAS5, SB5 and Ford R226. Stainforth ran all the Guy 'deckers, one Mark IV, five Mark V and one known as a Mark4½. The one Mark IV was WWX 671, a Burlingham forward-entrance exposed radiator example. I never found out what a Mark4½ was but ours, 7014 YG, had Roe forward-entrance body with 'Johannesburg' front. All the Mark V had Roe forward-entrance bodies.

There was the back half of a very old coach behind the old workshop and I asked Colin about it. His reply was, "I don't know, it was there when I started here". I asked Edgar who told me it was a body and chassis that had been put together during the war and was cut in half to make space for the new workshop. It was decided to cut up the remainder and I rescued a lot of old lamp fittings that had languished inside, I took those to Tony Peart at Haxey bus preservation shed knowing they weren't any good at Sandtoft.

I was allocated Ford R226 coach GYG 260J for my school contract until the coach was required for a private hire and replaced with a Bedford VAL which I found to be a very comfortable coach to drive. I only drove it for short distances on flat roads but was warned of brake fade on long downhill stretches. One driver told of pulling into a lay-by and pulling out again as the coach just wouldn't stop.

Wonderful Guys

During school holidays it would be all day in garage or all day on the road; Fleetlines were used on Armthorpe and Dunscroft services, Guys on Doncaster - Goole (known as Donny Goole), Ford coaches on Stainforth - Goole (Fox Goole as it started at the Fox pub). Fords were totally unsuitable for this due to their small turbocharged engines and frequent stop-starts. Clutch, turbocharger and engine failures were commonplace. My first service run with a Guy involved taking it over mid-route. I struggled with the crash gearbox and had to stop more than once. The conductress came banging on the cab back asking what the problem was. "George got his gears alright!" she remarked, George had been driving Guys for years. I soon mastered the gearbox and Guys became my favourite bus to drive. One Mark V, NWT 496D, had a particularly raucous exhaust and could be heard from quite a distance. I would drive this with cab door open when there was a wall on the offside.

The oldest Mark V, 891 GWT, came due for recertification, was taken off the road three months before expiry date and given a thorough body and chassis overhaul including repaint. During my meal breaks I painted the Indian's head motif, giving him brown face, red lips, blue eyes and multi coloured headdress. Doggy Wilson was very impressed by this. The Certifying Officer said, "It's a nice bus well presented, I'll give it five years, but I don't want to see it again".

Such was the co-ordination of the Armthorpe route that each of the three operators, Blue Line, Felix Motors and SYPTE, ran one bus each on Mondays to Thursdays, on Fridays they took it in turns to put a fourth bus on, Saturdays two extra buses ran on and Sundays they took turns to not run a bus.

Buses and coaches were parked outside at both depots next to main roads. One morning I got to work to find police cars in the yard. A PD3 had been stolen during the night and had demolished a concrete bus shelter; it had been towed back to depot and the front wheels were pointing in opposite directions as the track rod was bent. Edgar went to move said bus and Colin advised, "Tha wants thi left and right hand down". We carried out mechanical repairs but it went to Roe's for the bodywork.

One day Edgar had an aerosol can in the vice. Colin saw him and commented, "eyup Egga, tha's not supposed to puncture them tha noz", to which Edgar replied, "I'm not puncturing it, I'm sorring it in 'aif!" I learned a very good word at Blue Line, this being 'rammel' which means something that might 'come in' or might be useful to somebody else.

Private hire

Very little private hire or excursion work was carried out by Blue Line but I did operate a few, one involved taking Doncaster Civic Trust to see Lord Scarbrough at Sandbeck Park. The vehicle was LKY 133P, a brand new Bedford SB5. We had to wait for Mrs Wilson to address the party before setting off; she was late but announced, "I thought Lady Scarbrough would have plenty of flowers so I've bought her some chocolates instead". I hoped Lady Scarbrough wasn't on a diet. We were late arriving at Sandbeck and a Land Rover approached as we entered the drive. "There's Lord Scarbrough in his shooting brake", came a voice from the coach, "Oh, he's in his shirt sleeves!"

The National Coal Board provided much work for Blue Line in the way of pit contracts and we ran a weekend trip to London for their office staff. This involved picking up on Saturday morning, taking them to a posh hotel near Piccadilly Circus and parking the coach at Kings Cross. Collecting their luggage on Sunday morning and parking up again 'til returning them home at tea time. I ran this trip twice and was booked into the same posh hotel.

I once ran an excursion to Skegness using SB5 coach VWU 495L on a sweltering hot day, the only ventilation being a small signal window; kids were running about the coach so I daren't run with the door open. Another excursion was to Blackpool using 260J. This Ford overtook almost everything on the motorway.

Off the buses

After only eighteen months I left Blue Line to work as a fitter in Armthorpe Motor Company's commercial vehicle garage in Hatfield (the Yorkshire one). Armthorpe Motors were agents for BMC and Seddon. This was something completely new for me, I found lorries much easier to work on, less bodywork in the way and much cleaner, more room for muck to get away. The Goods Vehicle Testing Station was in the PTE bus depot and the first lorry I prepared for test nearly failed on its marker plates being covered in cement. I borrowed a wire brush from depot staff and it passed. This taught me to make sure such plates were clean.

I enjoyed MoT preparation work and realised a very thorough job was required; testing staff soon got to know my standards and often didn't inspect the vehicle. A local soft drinks firm called Heath and Smith ran a fleet of BMC FG's (the ones with the threepenny bit cab) of various sizes, some petrol, others diesel. They only came in for repair when they wouldn't start, wouldn't stop or wouldn't go round a corner. We often had to heat kingpins to get grease into then. Testing seemed to be an optional extra and when they did need testing we often swapped parts from another vehicle. We used to say "You can't make a silk purse out of a Heath & Smith FG". I was once tasked with converting a 900 FG (the six cylinder one with the extra frontal bulge) from petrol to diesel.

Blue Line WWX 671 was delivered in 1959 and is seem here at Doncaster's iconic Christ Church, the terminal point for many Independent operators. It was a Guy Arab IV with Burlingham forward-entrance body.

891 GWT was a Guy Arab V model, this time with Roe bodywork, and is seen here in Doncaster Road, Armthorpe heading for the quaintly named Cow House Lane. (*Dave Lovegrove*)

!977 saw a move away from the bus industry for a while when I commenced working for Armthorpe Motor Company. This Scammell was in use for a variety of towing jobs. Arthur Bates, mentioned in the text, wears a ginger wig for the occasion.

This Sherpa pick-up, HWG 334W, was use for the delivery of Bristol and Seddon parts and was for a time painted in Bristol livery!

TET 747S is a Leyland Fleetline FE30AGR with Roe bodywork. It was new to R Store (Reliance), Stainforth in 1977 and became SYPTE 1128 in 1979.

Blue Line ran two Leyland PD3s which had been new to Kippax & District. One is seen here a little 'off route' helping out on the shuttle service for the annual RAF Finningley air display.

The Reliance fleet included this Bedford SB5 (LKY 133P) with Duple 41-seat body, new in March 1976.

This Ford R114, HKU 795N, with 53-seat Duple body, delivered in May 1975, was also a member of the Reliance fleet and is seen here at Christ Church in somewhat wintry conditions.

A line up of Reliance and Blue Line double-deckers at the Armthorpe premises; left to right, a second-hand Leyland PD3A, a Guy Arab V and a Daimler Fleetline.

There was a lovely old man called Arthur Bates working there and I could write a book about his antics. Some of the heavier vehicles were fitted with Perkins V8 engines which rattled, clattered, speeded up and slowed down when ticking over. "Ticks over like a mechanical stomach pump", declared Arthur. One day a Bowater Scott van came in. It had "Scotties" written on its sides. "Look", said Arthur, "A wagon full of Snotties". Arthur had previously run a quarry with his brother 'our Bill'. One day he'd got a steam waggon stuck with its back end blocking a tram route. When a tram arrived he hitched a chain and it pulled him out, the tram driver saying, "I've got all that power station behind me". On another occasion he was driving an empty steamer downhilll where a bobby was on point duty at the bottom. Arthur leaned out and shouted, "No brakes!" Said bobby stopped all traffic and waved the steamer through. "He was waiting for us on t'way back though!" Arthur had also run a small garage/petrol station and lived in the adjoining house. Sometimes people would knock on his front door in the middle of the night. Arthur would appear from the back door dressed in white nightgown and nightcap. He would creep up behind them and frighten the life out of them, "They didn't come back again in t'night". He told us.

I once prepared a road sweeper for test but this was above my driving weight limit so another fitter drove it and I accompanied him. The vehicle had dual controls and my driver chose to drive it from the left of the cab. When he wanted to overtake he couldn't see past so I took over using the right set of controls.

Being Seddon agents AMC supplied parts to many bus operators including Crosville Motor Services who were unfortunate in having a hundred RUs many of which they rebuilt from dual to single door with parts supplied by Armthorpe who somehow managed to supply Bristol parts as well. One Sherpa van was painted in Bristol livery until Bristol found out and the name was removed.

And on again

I soon found I couldn't leave buses alone and returned to Blue Line part time. This involved driving colliery services two evenings a week. Following the closure of Thorne colliery coaches ran to many other pits in the locality. They would all be parked outside the Winning Post pub in Moorends between runs, where the service bus would pull up and that crew would also take their break. I was happy to do a Donny Goole afters shift on Saturdays as this guaranteed a Guy. On one occasion I had a problem with the bus and was given a PD3 as a substitute. The two PD3's were back-loaders and one passenger came banging on the front wing asking where to get on!

Blue Line sold out to SYPTE in 1978. Armthorpe became an extra workshop, Stainforth closed and the vehicles moved to the former Severn's depot in Dunscroft which was taken over at the same time. I was surprised to receive a phone call asking me to do a colliers run one evening. I turned up at Dunscroft and asked which coach to use. "Take any" was the reply, what an offer! Severn's had an AEC Reliance but that was on a pit, my next choice was an ex-Severn Leyland engined Bedford VAM, OWW 435E. I wound the destination blind to 'Evening tour' and this amused the colliers.

Amazingly during the time between take over and integration of the Blue Line operation two of the Guy's committed suicide on the Donny Goole run. Both ran off the road in the same place on the same day. One ended up on its side, the other remained upright but hit a tree. It was as if they didn't want to work for the PTE!

My next employer was Leon Motor Services and I'll tell you about that next.

Chapter Nine – Leon Motor Services

Iwas given notice of redundancy at Armthorpe Motor Company, the finishing date being October 1980. I heard that Leon were looking for a fitter/driver and applied there for employment. My application was successful and I started there immediately after finishing at Armthorpe but not before working one day for my future new employer.

The biggest day in Doncaster's calendar remains the St Leger horse race and the second busiest was the Battle of Britain air display at RAF Finningley, this being on Leon's service route. Every Leon bus that moved would be used on a special service to the show and many buses were hired in. Pete Goddard worked part time for Leon and suggested I apply to drive on Battle of Britain day. The Traffic Manager, Kenny Cockett, worked from an office in Doncaster's South Bus Station and I approached him offering my services. He took my phone number but I heard nothing for some weeks. With the show date nearing I returned to the office to show my driving licence and remind them of my offer. Kenny hadn't worked out the duties yet and didn't want to see my licence, "You know Pete", he said, "That's good enough for me".

I had to report to garage on the day, my bus was No 95, EKP 230C, an ex-Maidstone Corporation Leyland Atlantean and my conductress was Mrs Scattergood, another part timer drafted in for the day. We didn't run to a timetable; that would have been impossible. The instruction was to load to capacity in the bus station then join the traffic queue towards the airfield and do as many trips as necessary until queues had abated. A meal was provided in the sergeant's mess then return passengers to town as and when they started to leave the show. This continued 'til there were few enough passengers for the service bus to cope.

About a week later I attended my interview at Finningley, reporting to John Haydon, the recently appointed depot manager. I was introduced to the Managing Director Leon Heath, his daughter, Rosemary who was Company Secretary and his nephew Tony Rees, General Manager.

Music Bus

I was reacquainted with the Bedford VAL and Leyland Atlantean, the rest of the fleet being underfloor-engined Bedford coaches and Daimler Fleetline deckers. My duties were similar to those at Blue Line; morning and afternoon schools and garage in between. For overtime on Saturdays I would either work a 'music bus', taking kids to Thorne Grammar School for music lessons, or working crew operated duty 4 on the Finningley service. The former involved driving the last remaining Bedford VAL in the fleet whilst the latter was usually a Daimler Fleetline. Leon's conductresses were an amusing bunch; Grace Beedham was a laugh a minute. Once in heavy rain I was happily splashing through the puddles unaware of the water ingress further down the bus. "Jim, if you don't stop wetting my feet I won't buy you a tea in town!" came Grace's voice from down the bus. Another, Reenie Gore, had parents living opposite Finningley terminus and we would go into their house for a drink on our two 25 minute breaks on duty 4. I must have looked undernourished as her mother always wanted to feed me!

I would often catch the 7am Misson bus to work and one morning when there was a problem with the bus, it ran in to depot and clipped a loose chicken on the way. Next morning the conductress told me she'd picked up the dead chicken and taken it home whilst the bus continued to Misson and back without her, at the end of her shift she tried to pluck said fowl but it was so young the feathers were difficult to remove. Once out she roasted the bird and served it up but the meat was very tough. She stewed it and it was worse, then she realised it wasn't young, it was old, "but the dog enjoyed it!"

Down t'motorway

Another big event in Doncaster was the Miner's Gala. For one of these I was put on a private hire from the pit village of Rossington to Doncaster. I was given no route instructions so having picked up at the pit gates I set off towards town via direct. "Wheere's tha goin'naahthee?" came a voice from in t'bus. "Tha's supposed to go round t'village! Go down t'motorway!" There's a short stretch of dual carriageway in the village but I'd never heard it called a motorway before.

My move to Leon renewed my involvement with the Bedford VAL and LAL 547E is seen departing from Doncaster's Southern bus station.

An impressive line-up of Leon double-deckers in the depot yard at Finningley. Apart from the two Atlanteans on the left, which were new to Maidstone Corporation, perhaps the Fleetline on the extreme right is the most noticeable, with bodywork by Alexander to full Scottish Bus Group specification. The line-up had been arranged for a press photo to celebrate 60 years of the operator.

One Sunday I was given an excursion to Bridlington via the Humber Bridge soon after said edifice had opened. I asked if it went out or back via the bridge and was told either but not both. When loading I announced we would go over the bridge on the outward journey. One couple who were sitting directly behind me moaned they'd already been over it in that direction and continued to grumble for the entire trip. It was a very sunny morning but as I approached the Humber fog descended and little could be seen at all. I followed the road signs and they took me round the back streets of Beverley to the accompaniment of more moaning from behind me. Then the Minster hove into view and I heard, "I see why he came this way now". I was just following the signs!

In the workshop

I was put in charge of MoT preparations but they didn't like spending money and would cut corners hoping the Ministry man wouldn't notice, but he was there to look for such things and we obtained a lot of prohibitions. It was common to swap parts from a recently tested bus to one going for test but this was picked up when Ministry did a fleet check at the garage. Corrosion was a big problem with Roe bodies of the period and I was told to coat the engine bulkhead with underseal to cover the rust, smoothed on and sprayed silver two buses got through but for the third one I was required to stipple the underseal. "That's a fire hazard!" said the Ministry man as he issued another prohibition.

Reliable Gardner

All the Fleetlines had Leyland 0.680 engines except the newest 101 (HKU 361W), which had a Gardner 6LX and Alexander bodywork to full Scottish Bus Group specification, even down to seat covering and destination layout. I mentioned to Tony Rees that this came as quite a surprise to the enthusiast fraternity. "It did to us to some extent!" said Tony. Interestingly, apart from oil and filter changes, that Gardner received no maintenance in the six years that I worked there.

One of the Fleetlines developed a leak on the roof and I was the only one daft enough to get on top to reseal it, access being from a four wheeled gantry with steps on top of a box at its top. I got up alright and applied the sealant but found I couldn't get down again. It was winter and all the coach drivers turned up to laugh at my antics. Eventually one offered to throw me a rope but couldn't find one so an airline had to suffice.

Breakdowns

There were three Atlanteans in the fleet, No's 94/ 5 (EKP 227/ 30C) Massey-bodied PDR1s ex-Maidstone and 100 (OXS 14M) a Northern Counties-bodied AN68 ex-Cunningham of Paisley. The two Maidstone Atlanteans had been fitted with towing brackets and when one was withdrawn the bracket was transferred to 100, I told them it was at the wrong end as 100 would spend more time being towed than towing. The bracket was soon transferred to a Fleetline. 100 was always in trouble with mechanical problems so they decided to "Make it have it" and run it in all day service instead of schools. 100 objected to this and was soon back on schools. After its 0.680 engine expired I was required to fit a 0.600 from a withdrawn Maidstone. This involved changing the entire subframe and gearbox, thus converting an AN68 to a PDR1, well almost.

Leon's sister and Tony's mother, Dorothy Rees, was also a Director and lived nearby. If a driver had a problem with his bus out of office hours he would ring Dorothy who would come out to the garage, often in her nightie and dressing gown to pass on the message. She always had a cigarette in her mouth. On one occasion she announced she'd put some hand rags in our garage, when I looked I found a stack of newspapers.

I was on call for breakdowns (if I was ever at home to be called out). One Saturday teatime the phone rang and it was a driver with Bedford coach No 88 which had broken down on the way back from Skegness. I had arranged to see a friend for a pint or two but the breakdown had to take priority. I called at the garage and collected another coach that had just returned from a day trip, took it out into deepest Lincolnshire to find 88's alternator bracket had broken and fan belt detached, the driver had driven some distance without fan or water pump until the engine seized and coach came to a halt. Once cooled down the engine had un-seized although the batteries were flat. I topped up the water and got some of the younger passengers to push start the coach before they set off in their replacement. I then set off slowly with the broken coach. I stopped at Caenby Corner, parked downhill to let it cool down, sampling the products of the Monks Arms whilst I waited. After bump starting the engine on the slope and topping up the water level, I drove it as far as Gainsborough where I decided to check the coolant again but stalled the engine as I tried to set off on the flat. I was allowed to phone from a nearby shop but nobody would answer, it was quite late by now and the service buses would be due back in garage so I rang the garage phone which was answered by a driver who brought out a tow bus and tow started the Bedford but insisted on driving straight back. I drove the coach back on sidelights.

One Sunday morning Dorothy appeared with a message that coach 85, a 53-seater, had fuel problems on its way to Alton Towers with 51 passengers on board. I had only one spare coach, a 45-seater. But there was one more coach to go out, a 53-seater. I phoned the office and found 43 passengers were booked on it, I told them not to take any more passengers for that tour and switched the 45-seater onto it. I was just about to leave the garage when the driver turned up and demanded 'his' 53-seater. He reported me to Leon saying I'd no right to take 'his' coach. Leon told me afterwards he'd told the driver, "it's my coach; it's got my name on the side!" The driver couldn't argue with that.

Ambitious with Bedfords

The Company became quite ambitious with its Bedford's, sending them abroad even as far as Italy. To improve comfort some seats were reversed and tables fitted. When I took No 97 to test in this condition I was told that it wasn't registered as such and the examiner started to measure the distance between seats and tables. The gaps were slightly too short but I was allowed to adjust them, then the seat spacing was insufficient and they too had to be adjusted at the test station.

Such was the popularity of the foreign tours that heavyweight coaches were tried on demonstration. One a MAN, failed just outside Doncaster and was replaced by a Bedford. Another was a Leyland Tiger; this was more successful and became the standard although 104 (VKY 541Y) was the only one bought new.

Ill health took its toll on my driving licence and I left Leon in March 1986, just prior to deregulation. It took four years to regain my licence and return to buses, which I'll tell you more about in the next chapter.

Chapter Ten – Wilfreda Beehive

As I related in the last chapter, I surrendered my PSV licence in 1986 due to ill health. This was double vision, not recommended when driving a bus. Eventually I was declared fit to work but not PSV driving. I was classed as disabled and sent on a training course in mechanical engineering at Sheffield where they discovered that I knew no metric measurements. They didn't accept that thou's and hundredweights were metric; so I was put in a room with a text book and a note book and told to teach myself metric, this didn't work. The instructor spent more time playing on a computer than instructing. We were left to our own devices but a fellow trainee had been a welder and helped me improve my welding skills. I learned a lot from him and put it to good use at Sandtoft.

At the end of that course I was offered a place on a nine-month residential course at Mansfield. This proved much more interesting and I ended up with more City & Guilds certificates in mechanical engineering but whilst I was on this course my PSV licence was restored.

Wilfreda Beehive

At the end of the course I took a job as a driver with Wilfreda Beehive who had started competitive stage carriage work. I chose this operator because shifts were mostly between 7am and 7pm, late and Sunday shifts being covered by part-timers. My driving assessment was taken on a Leyland Leopard semi-coach, WCK 136V. The Leopard, despite being in production for more than my working life, had previously eluded me. I started in January 1990 and for route learning I was whisked round in a car, then they had a school to cover and I ran it. I took a driving job because I decided I'd had enough filthy spanner work. Of course, the filthy spanner work continued at Sandtoft and still does.

I found out how much bus work had changed since deregulation. We were competing with South Yorkshire's Transport, as the PTE's operating arm had become, and Yorkshire Traction. I soon found that other operators' drivers wouldn't wave to you nor let you out of a lay-by or road end. Some wouldn't even speak to you in the bus station cafes. I started by letting out other buses as had always been the case and persuaded other Wilfreda drivers to do likewise. Eventually SYT and YT drivers started to return the favour and we all started to work together. Some drivers wouldn't reciprocate and some were downright awkward and would perform dangerous acts to get in front of a Wilfreda bus, but they were a small minority.

Shifts were ten or more hours long, six days a week but schedules were quite slack and there was plenty of standing time on most routes. On my first day I had a short shift, about eight hours, and I was asked to do an emergency railway replacement to Sheffield using a Fleetline 'decker calling at all stations; I did this and worked about twelve hours. One route, the 178 to Woodlands, ran with one bus every seventy-two minutes; trying to explain this to passengers was very difficult, when told it ran every hour and twelve minutes they would say "Every hour?", "No, every hour and twelve minutes", "Every twelve minutes?", No, every hour and twelve" "Twelve minutes past every hour?", "No, every seventy-two minutes!" that just baffled them.

The Cub

A PTE tendered route ran between Hatfield Town End and Stainforth Station passing every back door on the way. The vehicle used was C923 DKR, a HTI-bodied Leyland Cub; the front-engined one based on the Terrier chassis. What a contraption that was, it was too big for the route to start with and spent most of its time with two wheels on the pavement. The floor was high and a staircase rose from the platform to avoid the engine. If (when) the Cub was off the road a Dodge S56 bread van was borrowed from Kettlewell of Retford. The Cub was bad but those were worse, everything shook and rattled; the worst buses I'd ever driven but passenger access was easier. Occasionally a VW Transporter twelve-seater was used; it had a passenger-operated sliding door and was totally unsuitable for one man operation. Eventually a new Mercedes Benz nineteen-seat minibus, H511 SWE, was purchased and the Company lost the contract. The

This Leyland Cub was photographed at Hatfield and Stainforth Station. I have explained its unsuitability for the service elsewhere. I was to renew my association with the locality, however, during my eleven week holiday, of which more later. The colliery in the background was the last in South Yorkshire and finally closed in 2015.

The replacement for the Cub was this Mercedes-Benz minibus, which is also seen at Stainforth.

Wilfreda Beehive eventually bought some Dennis Darts for services, and 92 (K945 JWE) is captured in the bus turning circle at Great Houghton.

Wilfreda also obtained this Daimler CCG, with Roe body and new to Darlington Corporation. It was used for Private Hire work, and is seen here at Sandtoft.

The company also purchased Roeville Tours, who owned this former Pontypridd UDC AEC Regent V and which passed to Wilfreda.

Among the other second-hand double-deck acquisitions was this Daimler Fleetline which had been new to West Midlands PTE. It is seen here at Old Denaby on a South Yorkshire PTE contracted service.

Cub then found its way onto ordinary service, a nightmare for the driver in high summer as it had a manual gearbox and, with very little ventilation in the cab, it was a sweat box. The Great North Road was being improved causing long traffic queues. By this time we were getting on well with most SYT drivers and I would tell them, "I want no laughing at me having this thing," and threaten them with, "I'll tell my Mam if you do and my Mam's bigger than your Mam"!

Nationals

Other services were run mainly by Leyland Nationals, dual-doored ones from Bristol. They were prone to smoke badly as the engines wore and one was banned from both bus stations in Doncaster so they put it on a route that ran into Rotherham before it was banned there as well. Wheelchair accessible services were won on tender and three Nationals were converted with a lift in the centre door well, clamps replacing seats in the front, lower section. Two were required for the operation and one spare. The spare frequently found its way onto stage carriage routes where passengers would pay their fare then notice the lack of seats. I had a number of answers as to where the seats had gone such as, "Well, they'll pinch owt these days; they were there when I parked up for dinner"! or "It's a new bus and they haven't finished building it yet"! One National, No 66, ex-Bristol, was sent to East Lancs Coach Builders and converted to Greenway specification with Gardner engine and rebuilt bodywork. This was also to wheelchair specification but a full set of seats could be quickly fitted for normal service. The National was an ideal tool for competitive routes, its uncluttered entrance meant passengers could board as others were alighting. It was common for a Scania coach to be used on service, not really practical as there was no ticket machine mounting. It had to be hand held and it took passengers too long to climb aboard then get into and out of the seats. They would say, "This is a nice bus, are we going to the sea side?"

Almex ticket machines were replaced by electronic Wayfarers; surely the machines were worth more than the Nationals. My training on this machine lasted about two minutes before going out on service one morning.

'Deckers

Wilfreda owned 304 VHN, an ex-Darlington Daimler CCG, the one with a Guy constant-mesh gearbox, supposedly for driver training but as far as I know no such duties were carried out. Chris Proctor worked part time for WB and arranged to borrow the Daimler for Sandtoft Gathering 1993. He drove it to the Museum and parked it on the stand for me to take out on an Isle of Axholme tour. It filled up instantly and this was my first time in the cab. Mike Hirst was my conductor. I found that it was necessary to just catch top gear when changing up from third or the bus would lose too much momentum. On return I remarked to Mike, "By, I enjoyed that but I don't know how we coped with them in service", thinking of the Blue Line Guys. Then I opened the bonnet and said, "There's the problem, it's a five potter", I had been used to 6LW engines in the Guys. I was fortunate enough to drive this vehicle several times after that before the bus was loaned to Dover Transport Museum. The Company later bought Roeville Tours and with that came an AEC Regent V, ETG 373C, new to Pontypridd Urban District Council, and I managed to borrow that from time to time for Sandtoft work. The Company ran three other 'deckers, all Daimler Fleetlines, but one day a notice appeared that none had to run after midnight that day. We were told that the Ministry had put a stop to their use as they wouldn't fit into the workshop. I never found out how they got away with running the Roeville one or the several 'deckers operated since.

Night Life

One late service that had run for years on Saturdays was the Night Life Express with one bus running empty to each of Retford and Gainsborough to pick up revellers and take them to a Doncaster night club. A £5 fare included admission to the club. We had to leave punters on the bus, collect tickets from the admission desk then issue them on the vehicle. The pick-ups were at 9pm, returning at 2.15am then we ran empty back to depot. On summer evenings the sun was setting on the inward journey and rising as we returned them home. These were the only times I've ever been in a night club. As far as I know this service still runs.

As more work was won on tender early and late shifts became the norm. Route 263 ran from Rotherham to Killamarsh, later changed to Eckington. To get the buses to and from Rotherham journeys from Doncaster were registered, continuing to Skellow near the Company base. All last buses left Doncaster at 11pm at that time and Wilfreda registered an 11.30 departure to Skellow. This proved so popular at weekends that a duplicate had to be provided. Early and late journeys to Barnsley on the 212 route meant starts as early as 03.50 and midnight finishes. I soon found I preferred starting work at 4am than finishing at that time. A night man was employed and he would, unofficially, run early and late staff buses.

To operate these contracts four new Dennis Darts were purchased and after a week of driving these it started to rain. I searched the cab for a wiper switch; it wasn't on the dashboard or steering column as far as I could see. I wondered if it was pedal operated but it wasn't. It wasn't raining much so I carried on without them; back in the bus station another driver had found the switch on the indicator stalk!

Bus wars

Management wanted to go onto a route that was already 'over-bussed' so that the opposition couldn't put extras on. The chosen route was Beckett Road but extended beyond the traditional terminus into a large housing estate previously unserved by bus, where residents had been asking for a bus service for years to no avail. SYT's response was to put minibuses onto its Beckett Road route, still to the original terminus and later to divert a longer route, Clay Lane, round the estate but those passengers stayed loyal to Wilfreda. Rumour had it that we were to use the Darlington Daimler on that route and, to beat us to it, SYT hired a Routemaster from Scarborough & District and ran it on the route five minutes ahead of Wilfreda which ran Nationals from the start.

A bus war broke out when Wilfreda registered on Lothian Road (Intake) every ten minutes. Again minibuses were the response, these extended into an estate beyond the terminus. This time the normal service was also retained so a bus ran on that route about every minute. Dirty tactics were employed on both sides including stand blocking by either operator; running boards were ignored. The route started outside SYT's town office on Duke Street and passed their depot. We would pull up at the depot stop if drivers were waiting, some would board the bus but many wouldn't.

I always enjoyed a laugh with passengers and when a woman asked for "Next stop please", I replied in a serious voice, "I don't stop here on Fridays". She wasn't impressed and threatened to report me. I said there was no need as it was Thursday and I would be stopping anyway. She laughed and hit me with her umbrella. As now the PTE set the child fare, then 5p per journey. They increased it to 10p overnight and next day two young girls boarded and one asked the fare, "ten pence" I replied then added "for you, and ten for your sister". "She's not my sister, she's my friend". "That's a pity", I said "It's 10p for sisters but 20p for friends". They saw the funny side, paid their 10ps and thanked me as they alighted.

Schedules were tightened up and standing time reduced, mileage was lost and drivers were having medical problems. As if sixty hours a week wasn't enough we were expected to work our days off and after working 77 hours, 52 minutes in a week I decided that was two week's work and left Wilfreda Beehive in July 1993 having enjoyed my three and a half years there.

Chapter Eleven – Yorkshire Traction

In July 1993 I applied for a driver's job at Yorkshire Traction (Tracky) when on standing time in the North Bus Station whilst working for Wilfreda. I collected an application form, filled it in and left it with my good friend Chris Palmer who was a Traffic Clerk. I saw the Depot Manager, Ian Kaye, on my meal break; he didn't conduct a formal interview saying he knew enough about me already. I was instructed to report to Head Office at Barnsley for a medical and driving assessment. This I did on my next day off and was taken for a drive in an ex-Scottish Bus Group Leyland Leopard with Alexander Y Type body, Leyland 'half and half' gearbox, ie crash on 1st and 2nd, synchromesh 3rd and top and no power steering. That was no problem to me, of course, but I thought it might put off new starters if they thought they'd have to drive them in service.

I was 43 years old and decided this would be my last move. I joined the pension fund, union and death levy. The last being a scheme where a small amount was deducted from wages and paid to the relatives of those who died in service. I paid into that scheme for many years but received nothing from it!

Three days type training were allocated, the first with a Y Type Leopard and two other trainees, a minibus driver hoping to upgrade and a lorry driver wishing to be a bus driver. Round and round the housing and industrial estates of Wombwell we went, up and down the box. On the second day we used a Leopard /Plaxton coach with semi-automatic transmission that had suffered fuel trouble and we were to test it. On the third day I was asked to drive a Scania coach in National Express livery down the motorway to the Scania dealer at Worksop, the training bus would pick me up.

The instructor, Brian Davis, was excellent, none of the bullying of earlier years. Some of Brian's words are still with me, such as, "you can swing your front overhang over t'pavement, provided nobody's stood there of course, if anybody is you don't do it". More words of wisdom were, "if nobody else wants t'road you might as well use all of it". In other words, take a wide swing on left hand corners and short cut on right ones. I thoroughly enjoyed the three days but doubted I'd drive any of those vehicles again, which I didn't.

So on the Thursday I reported to Doncaster for route learning. I was told I'd got locker 13 and given four different keys. I had three lockers all numbered 13 and a key for the locker room door. I was also issued with a Pendamatic, more of which later. I already knew some routes but had to learn the minibus routes that used all the side streets imaginable. I had to start as a minibus driver on reduced pay 'til there was a vacancy for a big bus driver on full pay; this would be two years. The agreement at the time was that big buses finished at 9pm and didn't work Sundays. Mini's took over for the rest of the time so runs to Barnsley and Wakefield were included. New drivers were only allowed to drive minibuses but those starting with full licenses could drive anything and be paid full rate for the duration. During my first day of route learning I was asked to operate a service journey as no other driver was available.

Minibuses were MCW Metroriders, short and long ones, and Mercedes Benz 811D with a variety of bodywork. Single-deckers were Dennis Dart bodied by Wright, Scania K93 also Wright-bodied and Leyland National 2. Double-deckers were all ECW-bodied Leyland Olympian. I found the Markk2 National preferable to the Mark1, somehow they seemed more solid, and I liked driving Olympians.

When my staff pass arrived it was valid on all Traction Group Companies; Lincolnshire Road Car, Barnsley & District, Yorkshire Terrier in Sheffield and Strathtay Scottish. It was also valid on the successors of the two PTE operators and the former National Bus Company operators in and surrounding our area. This was the first one of these I'd had for many years; again I put it to good use.

Spare duties

Early (4am) and late (2pm) spares were on the minibus rota. I liked spare duties as anything could happen, often taking or collecting a bus to or from the Central Works in Barnsley. Being in uniform I would wander round the various workshops without being challenged, always finding something interesting. I was once sent to Barnsley to collect a double-deck coach for a private hire next day. I'd never been in one of those before, let alone driven one. A cleaner had to show me where the starter and lighting switches were. I

The first bus I drove with Yorkshire Traction was this Alexander Y type which had been new to Western SMT in 1975 and was in use for training.

An offer of overtime found me taking a Rawmarsh based bus, M290 TWB, a Northern Counties-bodied Scania, to a bus rally in Leeds; passengers had been playing with the number blinds.

backed it out of the garage and set off for Doncaster. Nearing the village of Marr I checked the speedo which showed 70 and it was still gaining speed. Brakes were applied rapidly as I was approaching a 30 mph limit.

We had to collect our bus from depot in a morning then drive it to the North Bus Station to sign on. One morning I had to phone Chris Palmer before leaving depot, he had taken me off my duty. A coach run to Manchester had to be covered and he knew I would jump at the chance to drive it. The route was X60 and, in true Tracky fashion, it went via everywhere! I was given a publicity leaflet to help me find my way. Fortunately, I picked up an off duty Barnsley driver who acted as my guide. The vehicle used was a Plaxton-bodied Leyland Royal Tiger, of the B50 kind not the PSU, one of only three in the fleet. The service didn't last long.

Another unexpected run was one windy day when I turned up for 2 o'clock spare and I was told to take a Scania service bus to depot, have it cleaned and fuelled then go to Doncaster railway station. "They'll tell where you're going!". Overhead lines were down and I was to run direct to Peterborough as a railway replacement. The bus was fitted with a speed limiter and would go like stink up to 58mph then stay at that speed. When I got to Peterborough they asked me to go to on Huntingdon but that never materialised and I sat outside Peterborough station for about four hours before being told to load for Grantham, Newark and Retford then empty to depot where I arrived at about 2am after somebody had chalked a sign reading "Lost- bus 275- £10 reward if found"!

One day I was asked if I wanted to work my day off on Sunday. Of course, the answer was no; "But you don't know what it is", came the reply, "It's to take a bus from Rawmarsh depot to a rally in Leeds celebrating twenty years of West Yorkshire PTE". Rawmarsh had the newest buses at the time. I couldn't refuse that sort of overtime.

During the winter of 1993 I was told by Ian Kaye that as I was the 'granddaddy' of the late shift drivers he would leave it to me to call the buses off if the snow got too bad; needless to say I didn't. A Sunday duty ran the noon journey on 'DonnyMex' a 222 route from Doncaster to Barnsley via Mexborough. It was sleeting as I left Don and the sleet got thicker the further west I got until reaching Stairfoot roundabout where it was thick snow. It took 40 minutes to complete the ten minute journey and when I pulled into the bus station I asked the controller what to do. "Nothing" came the reply, "t'roads haven't been gritted so we're not running anything". I sat in Barnsley canteen for five hours before being sent out on time for my second trip back to Donny.

Pre-war Tiger

Tracky had restored a 1935 Leyland Tiger TS7, No 492 (HE 6762), and I was twice asked to drive it on private hires. I didn't take any persuading, this was another job I couldn't refuse. After that I was able to borrow the bus for Sandtoft duties. To borrow the bus for Sandtoft a written request had to be submitted to the Managing Director, Frank Carter. Chris Palmer once took me to Barnsley in his car and he drove 492 to Goldthorpe, struggling with the gears all the way, it was a cold morning and Chris was unfamiliar with the 'crash' gearbox. I took over when the bus had warmed up and gear changing was much easier. When we got to Doncaster we had to collect a Dart and Chris chose to drive that, leaving 492 to me.

Later, to celebrate its 60th anniversary, 492 ran on service for four Tuesdays in August, just four local runs replacing a service bus with a driver working as conductor. Boarding passengers would bang on the cab back window trying to pay their fare. I was detailed on that duty only once but what a wonderful experience it was, driving an ancient bus doing what it was made for, carrying fare paying passengers. Being paid to do it was a bonus; I'd have happily done it for nowt!

The Doncaster - Kilnhurst routes were merged with the Rotherham - Conisborough to form a Doncaster – Conisborough – Kilnhurst – Rotherham service; consultants were employed and four daytime routes emerged with another for evenings and Sundays. Routes 293 & 4 took an hour end to end, 296 & 7 an hour and a half (First's X78 took 30 minutes running straight along the A630). There was a point where a 296 bound for Rotherham followed a Doncaster bound 294 for a mile and a half round the housing estates of Denaby Main. Duties usually ran all four routes in five hours with fifteen minutes walking time each way. These were 'big bus' routes so minibus drivers weren't trained on them. One afternoon the inevitable occurred and I had a full run to operate. I had a street map on the dashboard of my Leyland National with running board and faretable also on display as I attempted to find my way. A passenger boarded and asked if I needed help. I didn't charge her fare and she guided me round several housing estates. I thanked her very much as she alighted then looked at the map to find I was well off route!

Miner's footpath

After two years on minibuses I was promoted to big-bus driving, much better as longer runs were the norm, one was to Wakefield via nearly everywhere, though some villages were avoided. One duty involved driving to Wakefield, half an hour layover, returning to Doncaster for a meal break and repeating the procedure. We would have our dinner in the excellent West Riding canteen on the first trip and our pudding on the second. There were forty-two fare stages on that route and I found all but one, called 'Miner's Footpath'. I had to ask a passenger who told me the path had long since gone as had the pit it served. Another was 'King Roy Lane'. I didn't know there'd ever been a King Roy but it turned out it was King Royd mis-spelt on the fare chart.

One day, when bomb alerts were commonplace, North Bridge was closed to all traffic after an explosion on the railway wires below it. The railway network ground to a halt and gradually, bit by bit, the whole town closed. A temporary terminus north of the bridge was created and a shuttle service operated via the police-only slip road onto the motorway at Sprotbrough to another temporary terminus at Christchurch. I was on afters and had to report to garage for a run from Don Valley School. The only way to get there was via Barnby Dun. A run from Ridgewood school followed and I pulled into the temporary arrangement after that. By then the bridge had reopened but not the bus stations. I ran from Christchurch to Barnsley and all was back to normal by the time I returned. It later emerged that the suspected terrorist attack was, in fact, a pigeon that had shorted out the overhead wires!

Dennis Dart/Wright Handybus 417 (K417 HWG) leaving Doncaster North Bus Station on the last day of operation of that facility. Preserved Doncaster buses having a last play in the bus station.

Chapter Twelve – More Yorkshire Traction

Routes between High Melton and Barnburgh served a stage called 'White Railings'; I worked out where this was but didn't see any railings. Later a new driver asked the whereabouts of this stage and I explained it to him saying I'd never seen any white railings in my twelve years with Tracky, another driver joined in saying he'd never seen any in his 28 years.

Nasty accident

I was involved in a very nasty accident one afternoon in Swinton. It was school leaving time and a lad was standing on the curb-edge with his back to the traffic; he was 'showing off' to his mates. I was in traffic and, anticipating a problem, moved my bus, Dennis Dart 412, out as far as I could. There was a bang and I saw the lad lying on the pavement. I stopped the bus and somebody was with him before I left the cab; that person was a nurse who was driving the car behind. All traffic ground to a halt and a paramedic approached, passing all the standing vehicles. He was in the area and realised something was amiss. Police arrived soon after; again they hadn't yet been called. Finally came an ambulance. Blood was running from the lad's mouth and ear. I thought he was a gonner but the paramedic said he'd survive. "Yhey bounce back at that age!" After treatment the lad was taken away in the ambulance and the paramedic insisted on taking me to hospital for a check-up. Tracky's District Manager, Daryll Broadhead, heard of the incident and attended from nearby Rawmarsh depot. I was interviewed by the police and taken to Rotherham Hospital in the paramedic car; Daryll took the bus away.

Later, when hospital had finished with me, Daryll collected me in his car and took me home. I was too shaken to work next day but ok the day after. "He won't do that again", said the policeman when he took a full statement later. Apart from being hit by a bus in the first place the lad couldn't have been luckier, having so many medical staff nearby; he made a full recovery and I was exonerated.

Stupid fares

When all other operators had rounded their fares to 5p increments Tracky retained smaller values, the daftest was 62p. This was a very common fare and on routes with several different operators. £1 coins were often tendered, giving change from that required one of each coin and float soon vanished. There were 98p and £1.01 fares just to add interest.

We had to leave our Wayfarer module in our 'machine locker' when not in use. One morning I opened my locker to find a different type of module; I asked the early clerk what I had to do with this. A man standing at the counter showed me how to clock it on in the depot reader then followed me to my bus and I was given brief instructions in its use. Wayfarer 2 machines had replaced Wayfarer 1s overnight. The main difference being that the alighting fare stage had to be used instead of the fare paid. I managed all the way to Barnsley and almost back to Doncaster before I had to issue a 'special fare' ticket for 45p that wasn't in the machine. I spent several minutes trying before giving up and offering the passenger, "today's special offer, a 20p child fare", at least I knew how to issue that ticket.

Our mess room in Doncaster North bus station overlooked a block of phone boxes. About this time people were starting to acquire mobile phones and some younger drivers would phone these boxes then hang up and call the one next door when anybody approached to answer. One driver would let them answer and ask to speak to "her wi' t'red top on" or "him in t'brown coat", he would hang up as they approached the person he'd asked for.

Breakdowns

Vehicle maintenance deteriorated astonishingly during my time with Tracky and breakdowns became commonplace. One icy morning on an early to Rotherham the demister was blowing cold. With a good load on the windscreen started to ice up on the inside. Buses developed rattles and I developed means of quickly dealing with them. Entrance doors had a grease nipple at their pivot point and it became obvious that no grease had been seen for a long time; the joint became rusty and moved causing rattles. I would force the door open against the air pressure and tie a rag round the operating arm. Cab windows rattled awfully and I would slide a weekly ticket wallet between frame and glass, tear off the paperwork and stick the plastic to the glass. Internal handrails squeaked at their uppermost point. My trick there was to stuff pieces of ticket roll into the gap and seal it with a weekly ticket sleeve. It was as well we had plenty of running time on some routes.

One morning on an early trip through Conisborough my Leyland Olympian lost its drive, it just rolled to a halt with the engine running. I tried the usual 'switch everything off then on again" several times before phoning the depot. "Yes" was the reply "we've been waiting for that diff to go". I transferred my passengers and the tow-bus, Leyland Leopard L7 (CHE 536K), came out, coupled up and towed me back to depot. Because my engine was running I had brakes and power steering also. I could see through the tow-bus and I did all the braking. When we got back to depot I remarked to the fitter that I'd enjoyed the tow, "So did I", he said, "I didn't touch my brakes once; shall we go out and do it again?" That Leopard, by the way, was the depot van; if fitters had to go out for anything they used the Leopard.

Another breakdown I suffered was with a Dennis Dart. I had stopped in road works in Doncaster and it wouldn't move again. Cars could just squeeze between my bus and the temporary railings and then a coach came along. Between us we managed to move the railings enough to let him through.

One really cold morning when I was spare very few of the buses parked outside would start. I worked with the fitter to start each one in line. Drivers were told to ignore the allocation board and take the one we had just started, "Tell them which bus you've got when you get to town and they'll have to sort it out later". That way we achieved a full service with very little delay.

Second-hand buses

Tracky started to buy second-hand buses and many were allocated to Doncaster depot including five Dennis Darts from Edinburgh; they were like new buses, immaculate. Two Scania single-deckers followed from Dundee. From the West Midlands came a large batch of MCW Metrobuses, not pleasant to drive as the power steering would cut out at low engine revs, just as it was required to get round tight corners. We had to reverse up a slope in High Melton College, reverse gear wouldn't engage until about half throttle when the bus would shoot off backwards. Natural reaction was to release the throttle then the bus would stop and the procedure would be repeated until the bus stop was reached. More pleasant were some Olympians from Yorkshire Coastliner. A few Optare MetroRiders came from Trent and these rattled excessively. Other minibuses included Renault S75 from London; these were van based and very uncomfortable to drive.

Perhaps the most unusual second-hand vehicles were four 1987 East Lancs-bodied Scania K112 single-deckers new to a London Airport operator and purchased by Yorkshire Terrier before that Company sold to Yorkshire Traction. The four were transferred to the parent company and rebodied by East Lancs. They were dealt with one at a time and each differed from the previous one. Comment at the time was that rebodying East Lancs Scania's was understandable, but not using East Lancs bodies. A fifth rebodied Scania joined the fleet, this being a 1995 K113 from Yorkshire Woollen District, its original coach body had been burnt out. All these acquisitions had different moquette seating and, giving Tracky its due, it kept matching patterns for each style.

Managing Director, Frank Carter, was never one to miss a bargain. Two American-built Spartan chassis were purchased and bodied by East Lancs. I did manage to drive one of these when a Scania failed in Barnsley and that was substituted. Even more odd was a chassis that was found lying about at East Lancs. It had been built by Kirn, a successor to Ward Bros, and was about to be broken up. Again Mr Carter bought it and had an East Lancs body fitted. It remained unique.

The Company won a school contract requiring a single-decker and a Leopard/Y type came from a subsidiary Company, Lincolnshire Road Car. This remained in its former owner's livery of green and yellow with Yorkshire Traction fleetnames added. A retired driveress who worked as an office cleaner was retrained to full licence standard and issued with a uniform. She would operate this route until it could be

Yorkshire Traction 341 (F220 PPV) MCW Metrorider, ex-Ipswich Corporation, on delivery from Barnsley.

Yorkshire Traction 311 (H202 TWE) Mercedes-Benz 811D/Reeves Burgess undergoing a major rebuild in Central Works at Barnsley.

Now YTC 205 (1975 HE), Scania K112/East Lancs, was new to a London Airport operator, but then passed to Yorkshire Terrier and then YTC, subsequently being rebodied. Seen in Barnsley with the author at the wheel. Photo by John Myers who was Tracky's Finance Director at the time.

Now numbered 47955 (N203 VRC) by Stagecoach, an Optare MetroRider, was a former Trent bus and is still in YTC livery.

Now Stagecoach 29898 (1901 HE), Kirn Mogul/East Lancs is seen in Wombwell still showing YTC fleet number 208.

Numbered16938 (YM02 CLZ) by Stagecoach, Volvo B7TL/East Lancs is seen in Barnsley sporting YTC Centenary lettering.

For its low-floor services, Yorkshire Traction introduced a new livery of Yellow and Blue. This Scania double-decker (YN53 PAO) is pictured at Robin Hood Airport (the former RAF Finningley but now called Doncaster Sheffield Airport) on service X19, Barnsley – Doncaster which was extended to serve the new facility.

The same ex-Yorkshire Traction bus became Stagecoach's 15417 (YN53 PAO), a Scania N94UD/East Lancs photographed in Wath bus station.

Stagecoach 28650 (K413 MSL) is seen in St Sepulchre Gate West, the temporary terminal point for services after the closure of the North Bus Station. It was a Scania N113/East Lancs new to Tayside Transport. which was then transferred to Yorkshire Traction. Tayside was West Midland owned, YTC had Strathtay.

In a previous photograph one of the Optare MetroRiders acquired from Trent was seen in Yorkshire Traction livery but former 358 (N206 VRC) is now pictured in Stagecoach livery as their 47958 but showing both fleet numbers.

Stagecoach 28762 (L268 LHE) Scania L93/Wright Endurance broken down at Stairfoot, Barnsley with Barnsley's Leyland Atlantean tow bus in attendance.

Stagecoach 32486 (K412 EWA) Dennis Dart/Wright Handybus in St Sepulchre Gate West, Doncaster at a time when the bus station was closed.

worked into the rotas. Freda was occasionally required to operate a service run at short notice when the schools were off. A passenger once told me she looked like the canteen tea lady in her pink cardigan and I replied that she was the canteen cleaner. The bus was later converted for towing at Rawmarsh depot.

Doncaster Council decided to replace the two bus stations with one and closed the Northern one first; all buses then ran through the town centre in both directions. Five minutes extra was allowed on all round trips but on busy days it could take up to twenty minutes to cross town and many journeys were lost. Local services ran off one route onto another so it was possible for three buses or more to miss out consecutively on the same route. Passengers just stopped coming out for buses and routes were withdrawn as a result. A lesson in how to lose passengers!

At about that time Doncaster Airport opened and several routes were invented or extended to serve it. One was X19 Barnsley to Doncaster which was extended to the airport and Doncaster depot gained a working and a bus, a Scania 'decker in the new low-floor livery of yellow and blue. The route crossed Doncaster town centre in both directions each way, serving the same stop on Cleveland Street. That confused passengers no end. Why use the same number for two routes? we would be asked, the reply was it was one cross-town route but they didn't understand that. Running boards showed a stop number at the airport but none of the three stops were numbered. The route was registered as a low-floor operation and one day, when the 'decker wasn't available, I was given a Dart 41-seater. Then a fault appeared on the Dart and a 29-seat Solo was substituted., I had to leave passengers as there just wasn't the capacity.

Tracky's office and canteen moved to St Sepulchre Gate West along with many bus stops and the PTE enquiry office. The barber's shop I used was next to this office and one day when I was in uniform the barber, Bill, an expert in every subject, asked if I'd driven tracklesses. I explained that I drove them at Sandtoft but not in service. He thought tracklesses were marvellous, no pollution at all. "Doncaster had them but we merged with Rotherham and Sheffield and because neither of them had tracklesses ours were scrapped and replaced by Sheffield's cast off motorbuses". I didn't explain that Rotherham had run trolleybuses too or that eleven years had elapsed between Donny's finishing and the PTE taking over!

A real time information experiment was tried on two local routes, a display at the bus stop showed how long it would take the bus to get there, waiting passengers would observe the display and, looking at their watches, would comment. "By you're bang on time!"

Stagecoach

One morning in December 2005 my attention was drawn to a notice from Stagecoach. It read "We are pleased to announce that Stagecoach has purchased the Traction Group. The previous Managing Director, Frank Carter, wishes you all the best for the future". Mr Carter had been one of the management team that bought the company from the National Bus Company in 1986; he went on to buy out his fellow shareholders and became sole owner. The Stagecoach staff pass was very useful, valid on all Stagecoach buses throughout the UK and, officially or otherwise, most other operators as well. The Tracky fleet was largely past its best and many different types had been bought second hand. Not surprisingly Stagecoach buses soon started to replace our oddities, some of these were non-standard vehicles acquired with other fleets like the Wright-bodied Volvos from Glenvale which ran in their previous owners' red and white livery. The Barnsley & District subsidiary fleet was disbanded and merged with the main fleet thus blue and white buses appeared at Doncaster depot. Of course, no type training was given and once when I took over a late running Volvo B6 that pulled up on St Sep' blocking the road, I had to drive it to the next stop before I found out how to close the doors and switch off the hazard lights.

At this time we were suffering a shortage of buses and otherwise serviceable buses were taken to Sunderland, Chesterfield or Carlisle for repainting and re-trimming with Stagecoach moquette.

Just after the takeover a Dart I was driving developed a flat front tyre on Bentley Road. I phoned depot to report this and they asked whereabouts, my reply was at the bottom. "Is that bottom of Bentley Road?" "No bottom of tyre that's flat!" After an hour I phoned again to be told the bus was to be recovered to garage. Another hour later a huge breakdown tender arrived from a contractor in Mansfield and the driver set about dismantling the frontal bodywork to clear the towing equipment then removed the half shafts before lifting the front end and towing the bus to depot. The wheel could have been changed in a fraction of that time, and it all had to be reassembled afterwards, such is progress!

Pendamatics

One advantage of the Stagecoach takeover was that Pendamatic change machines were replaced with cash trays. The Pendamatic consisted a set of tubes, one for each value of coin and a lever to release them. If a coin was dropped in the wrong slot it would jam when the rogue coin reached the bottom of the tube. It was then necessary to dismantle the machine to retrieve the coin. My Pendamatic had no front cover nor plugs above the tube screws. I had it off to a fine art, using a 1p or 5p coin I could unscrew the tube, lift it slightly and slide the coin out above the release lever then tighten the screw again. All done whilst the bus was in motion! I never liked these devices and was pleased when they were replaced.

A batch of new MAN saloons was allocated to Doncaster and it was thought the depot's future was safe; my theory being the buses could easily be transferred elsewhere. We had always been told that the depot was losing money and in 2008 the inevitable happened and we were told that the depot was to close. "Don't worry lads", said the Union man, "Your jobs are safe, you can transfer to Rawmarsh or Barnsley depot". I asked how I would get there for an early shift or home after a late finish as I didn't have a car. "A staff bus will run". was the reply. I knew this wouldn't last long and asked for redundancy, I was told that it would be without pay as I'd been unreasonable in refusing the offer of alternative employment. I questioned this and with the help of Depot Manager, Sue Pickering, I gained redundancy with full pay, but only fourteen years' worth as I was one week short of my fifteenth anniversary.

Passing St George's Minster, en route to the new Doncaster Interchange, opened beneath the extended Frenchgate Centre in June 2006, No 449 (N109 CET) also carries a Stagecoach name and fleet No. 32933. This Northern Counties Paladin-bodied Dennis Dart was new to Yorkshire Terrier in 1995.

Chapter Thirteen – First Bus

Before asking for redundancy at Tracky in 2008 I applied to First Bus for a driver's job at Doncaster depot, this was where I had started as a driver with Doncaster Corporation in 1973. I was accepted after an interview and driving assessment. To attend the interview I donned a smart shirt and tie but noticed some interviewees wearing jeans and tee shirts and wondered if I was overdressed. "I like the look of you", said the interviewer, "You're old school; those young'uns don't want a job. They've just come to get their forms signed so they can stay on benefit". The assessment was taken in a Ford Transit minibus.

Three days induction followed at Rotherham head office. Our instructor, Andy, obviously knew little about the job as he told us things like, "First run trams in Croyden" (of course this is Croydon) and, "We run these for Transport in London" (Transport for London). These were written on a blackboard and there were plenty of other inaccuracies.

We, a mixture of new and previous drivers, were led out into depot and taken straight to the two Sheffield Leyland Titan PD's, still owned by First at the time; our instructor opened the cab door and explained driving such vehicles. "Why?" I thought, "they won't even be licensed to drive them". We then proceeded to the rear platform area and he explained bell signals. Again I thought why? Then he explained ,"It's in your theory test". Theory tests weren't invented when I took my driving test 42 years previously or my PSV test four years later.

Andy told us of the scheme where First Bus employees could buy return tickets for First trains at £5 return per train operating company. "There's nothing to stop you going all the way to Thurso on your day off then all the way to Penzance the next day all for £5". I realised it would take two days to get to Thurso and it would involve two train companies. Penzance could be reached in three days from Thurso and would involve four train operators.

Tickets could be purchased from any station and I would always confuse the clerk by asking for the most obscure places. Once in Manchester I asked for Barnetby and nearly missed my train as the clerk tried to find the station on his computer. In Peterborough I would often ask for Hassocks when I wanted Hertford, I once asked for Tooting and caused a long queue as he tried to find that one.

When the uniform order form had to be completed we were told to order blue shirts for Doncaster or Sheffield, white ones for Rotherham drivers. When asked why Andy replied X78!

Five keys

First use the Smith's Five Keys system, an American thing meant to improve our driving. The first key being 'Aim high in steering'. We were taught to remember the five initial letters by saying 'All Good Kids Like Milk', This took me back many years to my school days when we had to remember the Great Lakes by saying 'Some Men Hate Eating Onions', I well remember the saying but long since forgot the names of the Great Lakes. Incidentally we would be tested on our knowledge of the Five Keys frequently by the regulators.

After two days in a classroom I was let loose with a bus, well not quite loose as it was a training bus with instructor, Alfie Pratt, and other trainees on board. I had to drive this Volvo B10M with Alexander PS type body from Rotherham to Doncaster depot. From there I was to drive a Volvo B7 'decker to the interchange, as the bus station had become, leave it there and report to Duke Street for further training. During this training I found that the Wayfarer 2 ticket machine was set up completely differently to those at Tracky and this took a lot of getting used to. I also had a few days to learn the routes, most of which I knew but some I needed refreshing on. Only three routes remained the same as in the Corporation days save for now using the interchange. The three were Weston Road, Bentley and Intake. During my time with First, Intake was extended into a housing estate. Leicester Avenue, now called Shaftesbury Avenue, reverted to its original route and was later merged with Bentley to form a cross town route. Evening and Sunday journeys on Arksey also operated to the route I remembered. On my second day of route learning I was asked to operate an Edlington service as no other driver was available; history repeating itself for the second time.

First 60508 (H664 THL), a Volvo B10M/Alexander PS in Duke Street, Doncaster on driver training duties.

First 40504 (KIB 6110), was a Volvo B6/Alexander Dash ex-Yorkshire Travel in Doncaster.

First 37186 (YM53 EOL) Volvo B7TL in Advert livery at Goole Station.

First 69461 (YN09 HFH), a Volvo B7RLE in Park& Ride livery at Lothian Road terminus on route 66 to Bentley.

It wasn't long before a garage man asked me how long I'd been back; I told him I'd been away for thirty three years! People would ask if the job was the same as with my previous employer. My answer was that it was exactly the same but completely different!

CPC

Those foreigners who govern our country, but hopefully not for much longer, decided all bus drivers need thirty five hours training every five years in order to obtain a Certificate of Professional Competence. They kindly allowed this to be taken in five one day sessions and we were summoned to Rotherham head office to partake of this training. Sessions started by everybody round a table introducing themselves. Some told us the names of all their family and one gave details of his previous marriage and why it ended. When it came to my turn I simply said, "I'm Jim from Doncaster, been in buses all my life". "How long is that?" asked one trainee. "Forty two years" I replied. "Well if you've been in buses forty two years you should be telling them how to do the job not them telling you".

On my first session we had to guide a blind person onto the bus, one driver had to be blindfolded whilst another sat in the cab and directed him, telling him where the grab poles were situated etc. Then it was my turn in the cab and I got the man onto the bus but the instructor put himself between me and the blind man and spoke very loudly. Then he sat in the cab and showed us how it should be done.

On another session we were given a blank sheet of paper and told to draw a map of mainland Britain. My partner in this exercise said he hadn't a clue so I was given the pencil but I can't draw to save my life. We were then given a list of twenty First Bus operating centres and told to put them on the map we'd just drawn. I was away with that task having visited most areas of Britain. When the instructor looked at my map he stated, "I'll give you nought out of twenty for your map and eighteen out of twenty for your places". I hadn't drawn East Anglia or Scotland correctly so Lowestoft and Aberdeen were wrongly placed. My thoughts on this were that somebody is paying for this and ultimately it's the passenger.

Goole and Epworth

I was told not to bother learning the Goole route as I wouldn't be going there but I soon found I had a Goole to do. No problem until I got to the outer terminus and found the town centre had been pedestrianised. I had to ask a passenger to direct me round that section. The duty allocator, Dick Farthing, asked if I knew the Epworth route. First ran only one journey, inbound from Epworth, Monday to Saturday, I said I knew where Epworth was and found I'd been allocated that journey to work next day.

On weekdays the first bus to Thorne and Moorends left town at 5am. It seemed very strange to be working buses through town at five o'clock on Saturday mornings, just as the night clubs were turning out, picking up the sort of passengers normally expected on late night journeys.

Vehicles were mainly Volvos B6, saloons, Olympian, B7TL and B9TL 'deckers. There were also a few Dennis Dart and Optare Solo single-deckers. As at Tracky I found the Solo's unsuitable as low-floor buses, with the entrance behind the axle it was impossible to position the door close to the kerb except on straight sections of road, passengers always having to step from bus to road then up onto kerb in lay-bys.

No spares

No spare drivers were employed and there were no spare buses. When a bus broke down in service it was practice to transfer passengers to the next one and wait for a van to come out. If the bus couldn't be made serviceable at the roadside but was drivable we had to drive it to depot and wait there 'til it was fixed or it was meal break or end of duty. It was common practice for three or four drivers to be sat at depot without a bus. Similarly, if a bus was involved in an accident, however small, it would be taken out of service whilst the driver was interviewed and the necessary paperwork completed. This was bad enough on a ten-minute frequency but shameful on an hourly service as that run simply didn't operate.

Chapter Fourteen – The Final Episode

Computer training

A union man, John Loraine, asked if I wanted to join a computer training class. My answer was "No, I hadn't got one, wouldn't know how to start one and hadn't got a licence to drive one". "We'll show you how to start one and get you a licence." said John. After a few weeks my sister, Gwen, who lived in Hertford decided I needed a computer and with her husband, Roy, brought me their old computer. Now I needed to know how to start and drive them. I joined the training course and learned the basics; I must say I really enjoy writing reports such as this using a computer.

Eleven week holiday

When the railway line was closed between Doncaster and Cleethorpes for the entire summer of 2009 First won the contract to provide low-floor buses for the replacement of the Hatfield & Stainforth to Scunthorpe section. A notice went up asking for drivers. I thought it would be something different and applied. This was the eleven week holiday I mentioned earlier, I thought that there wouldn't be much work involved and I was right. Vehicles used were Volvo B7L saloons, the type with upright engine behind the nearside back wheel.

Day shifts started at Scunthorpe and did three trips to Hatfield and two returns, after were two or three round trips all starting at Hatfield, some running off at Scunny, others at Hatfield. Three buses were needed for the service and one spare at each end.At dinner time two extra spares ran on about three hours before the early spares ran off so four spare buses were available for three running. We had a Portakabin at Hatfield and use of the railway workers snap cabin at Scunthorpe. Twelve drivers were required in all and two co-ordinators at a time at each end. Independent coaches provided end to end cover and there was a spare coach at Scunthorpe. If the wind was blowing in the direction of Scunthorpe station it was possible to not only smell the steel works but to taste them. In spite of this it really was a most enjoyable few weeks.

Road works

One day when road works were causing exceptional chaos in Doncaster I had a Goole to do, followed by a Hatfield using a Volvo B7TL 'decker. It took me half an hour to reach the interchange from Duke Street, running time two minutes, then a further hour and a half to return to the town centre once loaded. I did my best to make up time but still ended up in Goole two hours late. Passengers waiting there told me they'd been waiting for two hours and I explained why that was. I left on the time of the bus after the one after mine and the passengers took it all in good spirit. The Hatfield run didn't operate.

I always enjoyed a laugh with passengers and one old chap using a walking frame would board and alight in Rawcliffe Bridge. He certainly got about, going to Doncaster or Goole, sometimes changing buses and travelling further afield. He would tell me where he'd been on his return trip and I admired him for his independence given his limited mobility. One afternoon I advised him not to get a speeding ticket with his walking frame, next time I saw him he said, "You'll never guess what I got? A speeding ticket"!

If children boarded dressed as witches, pirates or whatever I would say witches/pirates weren't allowed on the bus, then ask if they were good ones which they always were, then I'd say good ones were allowed on.

When children boarded with a sweetie lolly I would ask for a lick of their lolly. The answer was usually a resolute no but sometimes I would be offered a lick. I would say I'd have a pretend lick and thank them for their kindness. School kids boarding with their cookery tins would be asked if they'd brought my tea and sometimes I'd be given a cake.

First 50238 (YT51 EZX) was an Optare Solo in St James Street, Doncaster with my abode in the background.

First 40596 (YG02 BLE) Volvo B6 RLE/Wright at Lindholme having followed the circuitous route 67 from Doncaster.

First 34097 (T897 KLF), a Volvo Olympian/Northern Counties at a temporary bus stop in Doncaster, West Street during closure of North Bus Station. The vehicle was later rebuilt to single door and electronic destination, having originated with First in London.

First 66112 (R912 BOU), a Wright-bodied Volvo B10 BLE at Clay Lane terminus in latest livery.

First 61211 (NDZ 3164), another Volvo B7L/Wright 'contraption' in Scunthorpe on railway replacement during my eleven week holiday on that service.

First Doncaster painted Volvo B9TL 37230 into DCT's final livery in October 2013 to celebrate the 90th anniversary of motorbus operation in the town. To launch the celebration, Doncaster 22 was invited to participate, the view being taken outside the Civic Centre in Waterdale.

First 50235 (Y254 HHL), Optare Solo near Weston Road terminus in latest livery.

First 40505 (K945 JWE), a Dennis Dart/ Plaxton Pointer which has already been seen on page 65 with its previous owner, Wilfreda Beehive.

Trapped Pram

I was called in to see the Staff Manager, Bill Jarvis; I'd been accused of trapping a pram in the bus doors and it was to be assessed for damage before a bill was submitted for repairs. I was shown footage from the bus camera; a group of people were seen standing at a bus stop including one with a push chair, one with a four-wheel shopping trolley and one with a full size pram. The film showed the bus approaching the stop and doors opening, me checking if there was room for the push chair and it boarding, checking again for the trolley and loading it then me checking for the pram and politely informing the owner that I couldn't accept it. She is seen smiling and alighting backwards, we see her well away from the bus, the doors closing and bus pulling away. "She'll be hearing from us" said Bill.

An elderly lady was a regular from Thorne. She always had her disabled daughter with her and I often chatted with them as they boarded. One evening they approached the bus as passengers alighted on Thorne Road. The elderly lady started to run for the bus and fell on the unsmooth surface. A young man who had just alighted stopped to assist her and I left my cab to help. We got her to her feet and onto the bus but it was decided medical assistance would be needed.

The young man phoned 999 and stayed with the bus until an ambulance arrived; meanwhile I radioed control to explain the situation. Most passengers transferred to subsequent buses but I still had those for Hatfield Woodhouse and South Common. The lady and daughter eventually left in the ambulance and I continued my journey twenty minutes late. I was told to run out of service, dropping off until the last passenger had alighted. I was scheduled to return empty to depot so I picked up waiting passengers as the next bus would have been an hour later. Soon after a driver asked if I'd called the ambulance, "Thanks" he said, "It was my mam". She made a complete recovery and was soon back travelling on the buses.

Celebrations

To celebrate 90 years of motorbuses in the town First painted a bus in Doncaster Corporation livery in October 2013. Wright-bodied Volvo B9TL 'decker 37230 wore the final, purple stripe version. Its fleet number was abbreviated to 230 to resemble a Doncaster vehicle. They asked for Doncaster 22 to attend the launch and I was very pleased to oblige, using a lieu day. Three vehicles including 22, 230 and a new Wright StreetLite saloon assembled outside the Civic Centre in Waterdale, Doncaster. 22 was put in front for the run to Skellow which had been the Corporation's first bus route eighty years earlier, but nobody knew which route had been taken or where the terminus had been. I drove 22, 230 was driven by Norman Wright who had been with the Corporation and all its successors and the StreetLite by the aforementioned Alfie Pratt. On return from Skellow we all gathered at Doncaster Race Course for speeches by First Group Managing Director, Giles Fearnley, and Doncaster Mayor Ros Jones and a presentation by local historian Paul Fox detailing the history of motorbuses in Doncaster. This was a very proud moment for myself, and for 22 of course.

The end

In August 2014 my double vision returned, caused by a different problem this time, and I had to surrender my licenses again. I told the authorities that I was a bus driver and knew where I was going so didn't need to see but they wouldn't accept that. I was by then approaching retirement age and my career on the buses came to an abrupt halt. So in forty eight years in the bus industry I've seen many changes. Once buses were maintained up to a standard not down to a price. If a bus broke down, which was unusual and quite often caused by a puncture, a replacement bus would be taken straight out. Passengers were king and we looked after them. One thing I noticed in later years was the lack of discipline by young parents over their offspring. I would hear, "don't do that, stop doing that, sit down, I won't tell you again, stop doing that", repeated time and time again. When I tired of hearing this I would stop the bus and chastise the parent by asking them to keep their child under control for its own safety. I would often be told, "It's my child and nowt to do with you". I would reply that I was responsible for safety on the bus.